Anthropocene Communism

Anthropocene Communism

Land and Capital in the Age of Disaster

Paul Guillibert

Translated by Matt Reeck

VERSO

London • New York

This book was translated thanks to funding from the Centre national de la recherche scientifique (CNRS).

This English-language edition first published by Verso 2025
Translation © Matt Reeck 2025
First published as *Terre et capital: pour un communisme du vivant*
© Éditions Amsterdam, 2021

The manufacturer's authorized representative in the EU for product safety (GPSR) is LOGOS EUROPE, 9 rue Nicolas Poussin, 17000, La Rochelle, France
contact@logoseurope.eu

1 3 5 7 9 10 8 6 4 2

Verso
UK: 6 Meard Street, London W1F 0EG
US: 207 East 32nd Street, New York, NY 10016
versobooks.com

Verso is the imprint of New Left Books

ISBN-13: 978-1-80429-638-7
ISBN-13: 978-1-80429-639-4 (UK EBK)
ISBN-13: 978-1-80429-640-0 (US EBK)

British Library Cataloguing in Publication Data
A catalogue record for this book is available from the British Library

Library of Congress Cataloging-in-Publication Data
A catalog record for this book is available from the Library of Congress

Typeset in Minion by Hewer Text UK Ltd, Edinburgh
Printed and bound by CPI Group (UK) Ltd, Croydon CR0 4YY

For Éléa and Salomé,
who know all about the communism of life

Contents

Introduction: Cosmos, Production, and Anarchy   1

1. Communism and Multinaturalism   10
2. Capital Does Nothing in Vain: The Historical Naturalism
   of Karl Marx   36
3. Nature Doesn't Tell Stories: The Cultural Naturalism
   of Raymond Williams   90
4. Taking Back the Land: The Practical Naturalism
   of José Carlos Mariátegui   119

Conclusion: For a Communism of Life   172

Acknowledgments   187
Index   189

Now what he had taken for men of small stature but of grave bearing were penguins whom the spring had gathered together, and who were ranged in couples on the natural steps of the rock, erect in the majesty of their large white bellies. From moment to moment they moved their winglets like arms, and uttered peaceful cries. They did not fear men, for they did not know them, and had never received any harm from them; and there was in the monk a certain gentleness that reassured the most timid animals and that pleased these penguins extremely. With a friendly curiosity they turned towards him their little round eyes lengthened in front by a white oval spot that gave something odd and human to their appearance.

Touched by their attention, the holy man taught them the Gospel.

—Anatole France, *Penguin Island*,
trans. Arthur Williams Evans

For this world, New Tahiti, was literally made for men. Cleaned up and cleaned out, the dark forests cut down for open fields of grain, the primeval murk and savagery and ignorance wiped out, it would be a paradise, a real Eden. A better world than worn-out Earth. And it would be his world. For that's what Don Davidson was, way down deep inside him: a world-tamer. He wasn't a boastful man, but he knew his own size.

—Ursula Le Guin, *The Word for World Is Forest*

Introduction

Cosmos, Production, and Anarchy

In our era of climate change and global environmental catastrophes, is communism relevant anymore? At first glance, there are at least three reasons to doubt it.

The first reason to doubt the relevance of communism is the unprecedented nature of the present. The specific details of our era differ fundamentally from those that defined the time when communism and its principal theories were born. Our age is characterized by unprecedented phenomena taking place on a previously inconceivable scale, including global warming, the large-scale pollution of our air, land, and waterways, the depletion of water resources in key places on the planet, and the sixth mass extinction. It is in this new world, whose natural limits prevent us from dreaming of unlimited production, that ecological movements, inspired more often by anarchism than communism, have arisen.

For almost two centuries, socialisms—anarchisms, communisms, populisms, anticolonialisms, feminisms—have carried the flame of social emancipation. Since the nineteenth century, they have shared a cosmology, that is, the representation of a world held in common from which critical statements can take shape and projects can be set in motion. That world was populated by a host of *beings* that Karl Marx grouped into the category of "productive forces": mines and factories, laborers, colonies, resources (woods, charcoal, cotton, guano), animals (sheep, often English ones), machines (powered increasingly by steam), plantations and slaves, forms of technological and scientific knowledge, and a social division of labor. By "productive forces," Marx meant the collection of natural, technological, social, and scientific means that a society uses for controlling nature and producing social wealth. These forces brought about historical mediations between societies and their surroundings. They encountered one another in towns that had become expanding places of production and exchange.

Socialisms shared a common goal: the end of the exploitation of labor and the eradication of polities that reproduce class relations. To be sure, different socialist movements didn't produce the same analyses or strategies, but they addressed the same problem—the abolition of the exploitation of labor—and so, they agreed at times, and they disagreed at times. Yet, they pursued, at the social level, a common project of political emancipation that had first been sketched out in the eighteenth century in the philosophies of natural right—a project that the French Revolution had shown to be realizable or at least had legitimized as one possible future. In addition to a cosmology and a problem, socialisms shared a philosophy of history. What was novel in this was how it brought together a lucid understanding of the atrocities of capitalism and an optimistic vision of the future: the Springtime of the Peoples augured the dawn of the revolution and the good days to come. However, in the countries of the global North, recent evolutions in capitalism have accelerated the destruction of the labor movement rather than put in place conditions that favor the development of communism. Based on the globalization of capital, finance capitalism has participated in the logistical restructuring of the world economy. History has taken a very different direction from the one imagined by early socialists.

From an ecological perspective, the world in which communism was invented has also changed radically. Forests are burning, and the seas are gradually rising everywhere around the world. In Greece, California, Australia, Brazil, Southern Africa, or even in Russia, megafires are devouring lands inhabited for millennia. Moving forward, we will be living in a world of droughts and fires, of storms and floods, of tsunamis and nuclear accidents, of zoonoses and pandemics. The SARS-CoV-2, or Covid-19, virus is a good illustration since it is the intrusion of the nonhuman into our social lives. It brought about a form of *disaster capitalism* in which sovereign nation-states coordinated with one another to limit the pandemic through sacrificing political freedoms and opening themselves up to different levels of exposure to misery, disease, and death. This virus, like all the catastrophes that it announces, confirms the emergence of a "new regime of environmental regulation."[1]

After Hurricane Katrina pummeled New Orleans in 2005, the philosopher Isabelle Stengers began to call our era that of "Gaia's intrusion."[2] Gaia marks the appearance of new protagonists in the history of societies: hurricanes, viruses, fires, droughts. They are autonomous; they act and transform the world in unique ways. This is not to say that these beings have intentions; it would be absurd to attribute intentions to viruses or fires. But they have agency, or a power to transform the world, which forces societies to adapt their organizational methods and survival strategies. Without a doubt, it is the increase of extreme weather events that "ask[s] nothing of us, not even a response," which change our understanding of history.[3] In 2003, while the US launched a new imperial war to gain control of Iraqi petroleum, the SARS-CoV-1 virus made its first appearance in the global ecosystem. As Stengers writes, this intrusion of the natural world in social history is "a major unknown, *which is here to stay* . . . It is not a matter of a 'bad moment that will pass.'"[4] Still, the objection could be raised: there is nothing new under the sun. Saying that natural phenomena interrupt human history is to say close to nothing new at all. That the principal preoccupation of societies is the reproduction of their way of life through more or less conscious interventions in their natural surroundings is self-evident.

1   Jean-Baptiste Fressoz, *Happy Apocalypse: A History of Technological Risk*, trans. D. Broder (London: Verso, 2024), 121.

2   Isabelle Stengers, *In Catastrophic Times: Resisting the Coming Barbarism*, trans. Andrew Goffey (London: Open Humanities, 2015), 43–50.

3   Ibid., 46.

4   Ibid., 47.

But humanity has entered into a new era where climatic events that disturb the normal functioning of modern societies will continue to arise more frequently.

We now know that global warming and the frequency of natural disasters are caused by humans. The extraction of non-renewable resources, the consumption of fossil fuels, the production of greenhouse gases, industrial pollution, and consumer-culture waste are the social causes of the biosphere's destruction. The anthropogenic causes of global warming are tragic, but they also demand that we modify our behavior to preserve the conditions in which humans and other life forms can prosper. By necessity, ecology will become a principle of political organization for the contemporary world. We must acknowledge the activity of these natural beings and their effects on the social world. In other words, natural forces are not only productive forces; they can also disturb the normal functioning of societies through climatic events, or new virological intrusions. Nature's autonomy prevents its reduction to a simple economic factor. Because we know all this, we cannot pretend that the world that saw the birth of communism is exactly the same as ours. Communist conjecture did not envision strategies to combat what global warming unleashed.

The second reason to doubt the relevance of communism today is the uncertainty about how socialism can be realized today. It is true that communism has not had very good press since the end of the Soviet Union. That is understandable due to the authoritarian cast of socialist governments and the historical defeat of the revolutionary project in Russia. The vanquished rarely have the chance to write history in a way that shows them in a favorable light. But we can point to another hard limit to the past's large-scale communist experiments: their incapacity to manage the catastrophic ecological effects of the technological infrastructure they brought about. The symbol of this is the Chernobyl disaster on April 26, 1986. In our thermonuclear age, catastrophes are not plot lines in science fiction or fantasy novels but the results of a technological *dispositif* that forever threatens to slip from our control. A "new climatic regime" of global disasters was inaugurated with the Chernobyl catastrophe.[5] Socialism was helpless. Worse yet, based on an eschatology of progress and a belief in the lack of a natural end to the development of the forces of production, the Soviet Union contributed to its own demise. Here, we run into the ecological limit of one sort of communism, and the ideal of productivism.

It is undeniable that a productivist strain exists deep within Marxism. Based on certain texts of Marx and Engels, this strain was transformed into veritable dogma in state megamachines, which justified themselves through this productivism (Russia and China most notably). Marxism put forth a general theory of revolutionary practice, but it also has helped structure the relations of classes, nations, and environments within the communist movement. It would be wrong to consider it just *one* formulation among many others in the socialist project. For two centuries, Marxism has been the privileged theoretical and political space thanks to which the communist movement has been able to define the problems of contemporary life. This is the reason why the strategic discussion of canonical texts plays a foundational role in Marxism: this discussion allows practitioners to understand the current conditions of the class struggle in terms of a concrete analysis of the present. But this sometimes leads to forms of dogmatism that base indefensible justifications of reactionary politics on the authority of the text. For instance, during the productivist period, the idea was universally held that increased production would lead to emancipation.

Productivism is based on the idea that human well-being is dependent on our capacity to produce always more material and immaterial things so as to satisfy the imperious desires of the insatiable.[6] In short, the more completely societies dominated nature through technology, the more individuals would be liberated from the chains of labor. This pairing of the domination of nature with the freedom from labor is not, however, unique to communism. In fact, it is a typically modern trope,

---

5   Bruno Latour, *Down to Earth: Politics in the New Climatic Regime* (Cambridge: Polity, 2018).

6   Serge Audier, *L'Âge productiviste. Hégémonie prométhéenne, brèches et alternatives écologiques* (Paris: La Découverte, 2019), 60.

which can be found as early as René Descartes and Francis Bacon. The specificity of Marxist productivism rests in the idea that the development of the forces of capitalist production would lead to the conditions of a communist revolution. To be sure, in the most celebrated accounting of historical materialism, history is the necessary result of a contradiction between productive forces and the relations of production.[7] The former include all the means (natural, technological, scientific, social) that a society uses to appropriate and transform the material world. The latter are the forms of the organization of production, that is to say, the types of relations that the different groups of a society form among themselves to appropriate nature, organize labor, and distribute goods.

In its most popular versions, historical materialism has led at times to the idea that the appearance of new forces of production would necessarily upend the previous order, producing a revolution in social relations, and that the forces of capitalism would be pushed to their very limit and so would enter into contradiction with the conditions that had given rise to them. This economic productivism still rests on an optimistic historical philosophy that believes in a progress of rationalism embodied in the forces of production. To the extent that the forces of production substantiate the progress of science, they can only be the initial signs of social emancipation. When we study the ecological ramifications of the historical period in which this productivist vision took hold, we can only regret the time's assumption that scientific progress leads to social emancipation.

The third reason to doubt the relevance of communism in the era of climate change is political. Since the beginning of modernity, ecological movements have relied on other sources than Marxism. From the utopian socialism of Charles Fourier to the social ecology of Murray Bookchin, or the anti-industrial Romanticism of William Morris and the Christian anarchism of Jacques Ellul and Bernard Charbonneau, radical ecologies have run the gamut of theoretical concerns. But, as a group, they have been more influenced by anarchism than communism. All of

---

7   Karl Marx, *A Contribution to the Critique of Political Economy*, trans. S. W. Ryazanskaya, ed. Maurice Dobb (Moscow: Progress Publishers, 1970), 20–1.

this exists in a context of small-scale struggles against industrial pollution, ecofeminist strikes, territorial reinventions, queer ecologies, climate and antinuclear activism, and peasant revolts that did not wait for their theoreticians to gather and organize. If political ecologies and worker communisms have relatively distinct heritages, that is because the principal socialist organizations in past times upheld productivist positions, excluding a priori the possibility of tactical alliances with environmental struggles. Moreover, these histories emerged from worlds that, without excluding the other entirely, were mutually indifferent and were traveling toward different destinies. These worlds were anchored in the spatial structure of capital.

Capitalism rests on the territorial division of labor that authorizes the accumulation of value by the ever-greater concentration of the workforce in urban centers. The expanded reproduction of capital presupposes, then, a certain "production of space."[8] Colonized lands are held in reserve for extractivist appropriation of imperial metropoles where value is produced by the exploitation of wage labor. The urban space concentrates the bulk of the productive population, whereas the deserted countryside is inhabited only by the producers of agricultural goods necessary for the reproduction of the urban workforce. This territorial division of capitalist labor produces an environmental scission within the forces of revolutionary struggles. These struggles are based on habits, practices, discourses, and desires that are noticeably different. Communism is tied to the urban industrial world from which it sprung; yet ecological movements are linked to rural and peasant communities. From our regular contact with machines in the great urban centers, we began to dream of the masses taking over factories and ascending into power. Outside of the cities, a separate dream took hold: the reinvention of collective ways of living that were less alienated from the natural conditions of human existence. This opposition is partly a caricature, but it captures a certain reality. Revolutionary hopes are born as well from past disappointments. In this way, the heritages of communism and

---

8 Henri Lefebvre, *The Production of Space*, trans. Donald Nicholson-Smith (Hoboken, NJ: Wiley-Blackwell, 1992).

ecological movements are relatively different. While the first is attentive to the ways of producing wealth while aiming for the abolition of the exploitation of labor, the second looks to rethink ways of living on Earth while hoping to limit the destruction of the biosphere. These two aims are not incompatible. Their convergence is hinted at in the way that urban and rural worlds remain historically interconnected. In fact, their separation was never complete. Agriculture has become entirely dependent on industrial production for its machines; simultaneously, social life has remained so firmly linked to the natural conditions of reproduction that the urban world cannot completely ignore the rural world, whether in the form of community gardens or peasant soviets. In part, this book means to show that political ecology will be able to succeed only if it adopts a communist stance: the general flourishing of individuals is dependent upon the abolition of the material conditions of suffering (starting with the exploitation of labor—whether wage, unpaid, or household labor). But this goal must now be rethought through an ecological lens, which so often has been missing from the communist movement. Because the exhaustion of natural resources, the consumption of fossil fuels, and the pollution of ecosystems are the accepted material by-products of the quest for profit, there is no accumulation of value without an exploitation of labor that destroys the environment in ever-intensifying ways.

This book proposes a counterintuitive thesis: the ecological crisis does not push communism further away; instead, it calls for its urgent return. It is true that communism must shed its productivist trappings in order to become ecological, that it must reorient itself in an era of global warming, and that it must realize the utopian prerogatives of rural communes. But, if we agree to resuscitate communism, it must be as the "cosmopolitics" of the Anthropocene.[9] Perhaps a cosmic politics is a laughable proposition; nevertheless, it is undeniable that ecology involves beings that are "other than humans," and so new realities for political thought are open for

---

9   Eduardo Viveiros de Castro, *Cannibal Metaphysics*, trans. Peter Skafish (Minneapolis: University of Minnesota Press, 2014), 60.

consideration.[10] Whether to fight against the destruction of the biosphere, for the survival of the ozone layer, for the preservation of those species that can still be saved, or for controlling the spread of a virus, nonhuman interests in politics must be addressed. Moving forward, politics must also be conducted with a regard for beings that act silently. Acting in respect to their interests (the survival of the bees, for example) is also done in respect of our best interests (the need for pollination for agricultural production). As the public health crisis in the global ecosystem brought on by the spread of Covid-19 has shown, it is in our best interests that the environments of bats (one of the principal reservoirs of virological biodiversity) remain relatively unthreatened by human activities.[11] And it is the same for permafrost, virgin forests, wetlands, and other relatively untarnished natural habitats. But nonhuman ways of intervening are very different from ours. They do not unite in parties, soviets, or revolutions. Inaugurating an ecological communism assumes an understanding of the type of agency that is unique to life.

Communism must become ecological. And yet this argument is incomplete if it does not include its corollary: political ecology can become truly revolutionary only by becoming communist. This counterintuitive claim activates the seemingly archaic vocabulary of Marxism. Seeing this logic through to its conclusion requires us to understand what in communism's heritage we must claim for ourselves.

---

10   Ibid., 60.
11   On the connection between Covid-19 and the destruction of bat habitats by deforestation, see Andreas Malm, *Corona, Climate, Chronic Emergency: War Communism in the Twenty-First Century* (London: Verso, 2020).

1

Communism and Multinaturalism

> *Without the reptiles, the lagoons and the creeks of office blocks half-submerged in the immense heat would have had a strange dream-like beauty, but the iguanas and basilisks brought the fantasy down to earth. As their seats in the one-time boardrooms indicated, the reptiles had taken over the city. Once again they were the dominant form of life.*
>
> —J. G. Ballard, *The Drowned World*

The inception of the Anthropocene is a materialist event par excellence. This term is used to mark a historical period when social activities have left their traces in the ground and the air, have disturbed habitats, have destroyed entire ecosystems, and have exterminated hundreds of animal species. During this new geological period, the influence of societies on the ecosphere has become the predominate cause of the modification of biotic and climatic conditions of life on Earth in an irreversible way for humanity. Of course, the ambiguity of the concept is open to critique: it occludes the real causes of the ecological disaster upon us behind a vague universal, the *anthropos*. For example, we know that since the beginning of the Industrial Revolution, Mozambique is responsible for 0.2 percent of greenhouse gases, whereas the United

States is responsible for 20 percent, and Germany 4 percent.[1] Generally speaking, colonial ecosystems were devastated by a plantation system wholly geared to the colonizer's economy.[2] Profit-oriented industrial production, and so bourgeois capitalist society, in the world's rich countries is responsible for the biosphere's destruction. We know as well that women are more exposed to the health and ecological risks brought about by climate change.[3] For all these reasons, it would no doubt be better to speak of the Occidentalocene, the Plantationocene, the Capitalocene, or the Androcene. But, whatever name we choose and for whatever reasons we insist upon addressing it, capitalist production has undeniably transformed our environments and uprooted human relations from the material conditions of their existence. Collectivities, in order to adapt, must now deal with these new environments and modify their manner of production. In transforming nature, societies have transformed the conditions of their future; they have produced effects that now define the "natural" environment in which they are evolving. However, this "Anthropocene event" imposes a materialist reading of the climate crisis.[4]

The Materiality of the Disaster

In one of the most famous pages of *The German Ideology*, Marx and Engels define historical materialism in the following terms:

> The first premise of all human history is, of course, the existence of living human individuals. Thus the first fact to be established is the

1   Zetkin Collective and Andreas Malm, *White Skin, Black Fuel: On the Danger of Fossil Fascism* (London: Verso, 2021).

2   Jason W. Moore, "Sugar and the Expansion of the Early Modern World-Economy: Commodity Frontiers, Ecological Transformation, and Industrialization," *Review* 3, no. 23 (2000): 409–33.

3   For example, see Giovanna Di Chiro, "'Living Is for Everyone': Border Crossings for Community, Environment, and Health," *Osiris* 19 (2004): 112–29.

4   Christophe Bonneuil and Jean-Baptiste Fressoz, *The Shock of the Anthropocene: The Earth, History, and Us* (London: Verso, 2016).

physical organization of these individuals and their consequent relation to the rest of nature. Of course, we cannot here go either into the
actual physical nature of man, or into the natural conditions in which
man finds himself—geological, oro-hydrographical, climatic and so
on. The writing of history must always set out from these natural
bases and their modification in the course of history through the
action of men.[5]

It is striking how the Capitalocene brings back this materialist conception of history. The history of societies is the result of the transformation
of nature by pre-established modes of production. To the extent that
production leads to the transformation of a natural material into an
object fit for social needs, the structure of society develops from the
mode of relating to nature inherent in its production relations. The ways
societies relate to the environment transform the world, but these ways
also transform societies themselves, since their "natural" needs, their
labor process, and their organizational forms evolve as the environment
is transformed. According to historical materialism, the "interaction
between man and nature is, and produces, social evolution."[6] The
Marxist study of societies is the history of the material production of
their conditions of existence; the climate disaster demands that even the
least Marxist thinkers bear in mind this historical materiality.[7]

It is possible to state one of Marx's essential points in these terms: the
transformations that societies impose on nature modify societies themselves. A society that uses fissionable material to produce electricity is
different from the one that uses fossil fuels to produce steam. However,
the centrality of the environment to the history of societies does not
necessarily lead to an ecological perspective. It would, in fact, be possible
to argue the opposite: the presence of nature subdued by the demiurgical

---

5   Friedrich Engels and Karl Marx, *The German Ideology*, trans. William Lough
(Moscow: Progress Publishers, 1976), 37.

6   Eric Hobsbawm, introduction to Karl Marx, *Pre-capitalist Economic
Formations* (New York: International Publishers, 1965), 12.

7   Bruno Latour, *Down to Earth: Politics in the New Climatic Regime*
(Cambridge: Polity, 2018), 74.

power of labor would be, instead, a sign of a Marxist "Prometheanism," and so of an entirely modern belief in the human capacity to transform the world to reflect our desires.[8] However, if Marx is a productivist thinker, it is not in the usual sense of productivism, but in a descriptive sense: according to him, the structural elements of a society are determined by *the production of material conditions of human existence.* For this materialist conception of history to be adapted to the Capitalocene, it must be carried forward to its logical conclusion: if societies are themselves transformed while transforming their environment, then these environments shape the trajectory of societies. The social history of nature is inseparable from the ecological history of societies.

Abolition of Private Property

The second basic element of communism in the Anthropocene is tied to the first: social transformations of nature are always conditioned by *property relations.*

Generally, property relations are social relations between human beings that organize the objective relations of these people with nonhuman beings. Property is, then, a host of abstract and concrete rules that authorize in each society the type of relations that we can have with nonpersonal things, "nonhumans." These nonhumans are natural beings, technological objects, or products of labor. But this definition has a corollary: all social relations (between people) are mediated by relations with things. For example, in terms of simple private property, an individual owner possesses a nonhuman thing (some land, a factory, a patent). Ownership of this thing gives an exclusive right over possession and use, including its destruction. Whether formalized as an explicit right or held to be so by popular practice, ownership is a social relation because it presupposes a group of people who recognize the individual owner's right over the thing in question. Possession is different from

---

8 Serge Audier, *L'Âge productiviste. Hégémonie prométhéenne, brèches et alternatives écologiques* (Paris: La Découverte, 2019), 149.

ownership: to possess something (to *hold* it) does not mean the person is its owner; it is possible a person is keeping it on behalf of the owner, is renting it, or has stolen it. For simple private property, there is both a social relation (between people) that legitimizes the private and exclusive appropriation of a thing, and an individual relation to the thing from which all others are excluded.

Property's social relations construct how a person relates to a thing; this relation to things determines relations among people. The owner and the person who does not own a thing, for example, develop a relation that is determined by the possession and the absence of possession of nonhuman realities which are used according to the social norms of legitimate appropriation. The person *without* depends on the owner for what they need (conditions for subsistence, means of working, a place to live and to enjoy life). More precisely, for Robert Brenner, one of the initiators of "political Marxism," property relations mean

> the relationships among the direct producers, among the class of exploiters (if any exists), and between the exploiters and producers, which specify and determine the regular and systematic access of the individual actors (or families) to the means of production *and* the economic product.

He adds,

> In every social economy, such property relations will exist, and make it possible for the direct producers and exploiters (if any) to continue to maintain themselves as they were—i.e. in the class position they already held, as producers or exploiters.[9]

Several essential elements appear in this definition of property relations. First, they are the social relations that determine access to the

---

9   Robert Brenner, "The Social Basis of Economic Development," in John Roemer, ed., *Analytic Marxism* (Cambridge: Cambridge University Press, 1986), 23–53, 26.

means of subsistence and products of labor. Among the principal means of subsistence, the land must be counted, insomuch as the land provides the natural resources needed for the existence of individuals and collectivities. From this perspective, property relations are not reducible to property *rights*, although this right often expresses a concrete legal form. There are always real forms of appropriation that are not written into the law, whether because there is no pre-established framework to deal with them, because certain practices are illegal, or because these forms of appropriation undergo modifications that put the applicable right into contradiction with actual practices. Ample proof is on hand when looking at the evolution of the legal norms of the private appropriation of biotechnologies: the appearance of new sectors of accumulation leads to forms of "appropriation by dispossession," which are made legal by new rights in patent law.[10]

Second, social classes are the products of the relations of private property. Effectively, to the degree to which property determines access to the means of production and the distribution of the products of labor, the relations of private property fix in place the existence of producers and exploiters (if there are any). Exploiters are those who structurally extract a part of the wealth produced by the producers: this extraction aims not only to guarantee their means of subsistence as individuals but also to guarantee their means of reproduction as a class. For social classes to exist, there must be a structural extraction of the surplus labor to guarantee to a particular class the possibility of its existence over the long haul. By organizing access to the means of subsistence and in organizing the labor process and the distribution of the social product, property relations determine accordingly the existence and reproduction of social classes, which is to say, societies in which natural wealth, the labor process, and its products are not hampered by a part of the collectivity (or, in any event, not in a structural manner). While private property dispossesses a part of the community of its means of subsistence, the

---

10   David Harvey, *The New Imperialism* (Oxford: Oxford University Press, 2005).

collective ownership of the earth sets up, conversely, freer relations among people.

Classes emerge not only through the extraction of surplus labor, but also through the appropriation of the natural conditions of subsistence. The means of subsistence include the earth and all the natural forces that guarantee the conditions of life. The exploiting class is the one that possesses control of a host of natural forces and the means of production from which the exploited class is dispossessed (fields, forests, coal, harvests, uranium mines, factories). But an important point must be made here: the exploiting class possesses natural resources, or the *productive forces that allow their appropriation*. Those who own windmills and wind turbines use technological means to appropriate the natural power of wind; those who possesses hydroelectric dams can use the inherent power of water; nuclear power plants use the power of atomic fission. Classes emerge and are perpetuated as well through the appropriation of the technological and social means for exploiting nature. How we use nature is thus conditioned by who owns the productive forces, and the appropriation of nature determines the history of social classes.

Third, while there is no society in which ownership plays no part, *private* property—which can take diverse forms in history—expresses a very specific relation between people and things. In capitalism, for example, a part of the collectivity is systematically deprived of its relation to its means of subsistence; and so, a part of the population is thereby dispossessed of the natural conditions of its reproduction. Ownership determines access to the means of subsistence, beginning with the natural conditions of human existence. The history of classes is unthinkable if we ignore the history of relations with nature; the history of how we relate to nature is unthinkable if we ignore the history of social classes.

If communism is the best-suited form of politics to address the Capitalocene, it is because its central tenet—the critique of private ownership of the means of production—continues to be pertinent. Marx and Engels focused readers on this point in *The Communist Manifesto*: "The theory of the Communists may be summed up in the single sentence: Abolition of private property."[11] It is striking how many contemporary environmental struggles, and how much of the fighting done by indigenous peoples or in ZADs (*zones à défendre*, or "zones to defend") put the abolition of private property back at the center of political debates.[12] Today, this fundamental claim of revolutionary communism is being expressed as well in decolonial, ecological, and territorial struggles. Refusing to appropriate the land and its resources, these struggles place the occupation of space at the heart of the struggle against capital. They supplement the worker critique of the capitalist mode of production with an ecological and decolonial critique of its ways of appropriating nature. This is what a Marxist intervention in ecology can do: it can focus us on how the exploitation of labor, the colonization of the earth's land, and the destruction of nature are all part of the system of capitalist property relations, which deprives human and nonhuman collectivities of their means of subsistence.

The Ecology of Class Struggle

The third structural element of communism that political ecology must take up is the class struggle. Social struggles determine the history of property relations, just as these relations condition the degree of strife and the ways by which these struggles are manifested. When we think about the struggles against *enclosures* and extractivism, about demands for the self-governance of lands, and about fights over patents, we see how indigenous and ecological politics today confront the centrality of capitalist private property.

But it is not necessarily true that struggles against private property are class struggles. Generally, it could be said that these struggles bear

---

11   Friedrich Engels and Karl Marx, *Manifesto of the Communist Party* (1848), trans. S. Moore and F. Engels (1888; repr., London: Pluto Press, 2008), 54.

12   [Translator's note: "ZAD", for "zone à défendre" (zone to defend), is a neologistic acronym describing a conflict zone in which developers and local people confront each other over different visions of land use. The most famous case in France is that of Notre-Dame-des-Landes, near Nantes in western France.]

principally on the organization of labor: its mechanical division inside businesses, the legal length of the workday, the pay scale that it implements. But the organization and the division of labor depend on property relations. Working conditions are fundamentally determined by the ownership of the means of production and subsistence. For example, the legal length of the workday in contemporary societies is at the heart of a conflict between the "direct" producers (unions and labor collectivities) and those who own the means of production (represented by the owners of businesses). The organization of labor is determined by the social relations that fix in place who owns the means of production. At the same time, we cannot reduce class struggles to struggles over the organization of labor (as important as the latter are). Class struggles involve, by extension, all the struggles relative to land ownership, the means of production, and the products of labor.

An indigenous struggle against extractivist appropriation of the land and the worker struggle against the exploitation of wage labor are sometimes a part of the same struggle against property relations, which structure the dispossession of the means of subsistence. Ecological Marxism seeks to address the environmental conditions of the exploitation of labor, but also the centrality of human-nature relations in the structure of classes themselves. In sum, conflicts over the use and appropriation of nature have always been at the center of class struggle.

In a series of articles from 1842, Marx presented this point in a striking manner. To be sure, Marx was not yet fully Marxist; in 1842, he had not yet set forth the fundamental concepts of historical materialism. Nevertheless, the problem of human-nature relations within class relations was already sketched out in his writings, where he analyzed the Rhine Assembly's legislation concerning the "theft of wood."[13] This 1842 law aimed to reinforce the power of local property owners over their land by banning peasants from using the forests. This case shows the

---

13   Karl Marx, "Proceedings of the Sixth Rhine Province Assembly," in Daniel Bensaïd, *The Dispossessed: Karl Marx's Debates on Wood Theft and the Right of the Poor*, trans. Robert Nichols (Minneapolis: University of Minnesota Press, 2021), 59–106.

conflict between the customary rights of use—which guaranteed to peasants the conditions of minimal subsistence in that period of the rapid expansion of the proletariat—and property rights, which aim to exclude everyone who is not an owner from the enjoyment of natural goods. The law aimed to curtail *the use of the land* and to implement the *private ownership of land*. The debates in the assembly covered two technical points: Is dead wood that has fallen from trees the property of the tree's owner, or is it a common good from which anyone can benefit? Then, should those who pick up the wood be subject to forest laws and monetary fines, or should the law that treats theft be applied with its criminal punishments (escalating to forced labor) on behalf of the injured party, the owner?

Marx's response followed two lines of argumentation characteristic of his liberal period but that announced his imminent passage into socialism. On the one hand, it is impossible to consider that picking up fallen wood is a theft of wood since "[the] thief carries his own authority to cast judgment against property. The gathering of twigs is merely to execute the judgment already rendered by nature itself: you only possess the tree, the tree no longer possesses the branches in question."[14] On the other hand, Marx expanded critiques of the scapegoating of peasants to include a critique of private property in general. Relations with nature are conditioned by property relations, which are the object of class struggle. Ownership confers power to certain social groups by giving them control over resources. The appropriation of nature appears then as a condition and a means of social domination. This is the reason why struggles for access to land are an essential motif in the history of classes. Each fight against the capitalist dispossession of land consequently bears upon the class structure of property relations in a fundamental way. Seen in this light, the reappropriation of land in ecological and decolonial struggles acquires a new dimension.

These movements are generally against capitalist extractivism and the colonial or postcolonial land seizures that set it in motion. They envision other relations to land and other uses of resources. We can point to how

---

14   Ibid., 62.

some anti-extractivist indigenous movements today are reinventing the meaning of communism on the basis of ecological cosmologies. In its ecological bearings, the community appears as the effect of social interactions between humans and nonhumans. In its communist comportment, it fights against private property, which authorizes the monopolization of the means of subsistence, by proposing forms of collective ownership. We find a perfect example of this in the struggle of native peoples, for example, the Oceti Sakowin (the "Great Sioux Nation," in American colonial vocabulary) at Standing Rock in the United States. This "decolonial ecology" is not reducible to the class struggle, but it nevertheless manifests a certain number of its structural elements, beginning with a critique of private property.[15]

Standing Rock is a reservation where Lakota members of the Oceti Sakowin Oyate live. Since the 1970s, it has welcomed the first international conferences of indigenous peoples, and since 2016 it has become known as one of the symbols of struggles against extractivism. The construction of the Dakota Access Pipeline (DAPL) began in 2014; the project foresaw a new 1,800-kilometer pipeline carrying more than 500,000 barrels of oil per day from North Dakota. The pipeline had to skirt the reservation's northern border, and yet the land that it planned to cross would nevertheless have been Lakota land, as provisioned by the treaties of Fort Laramie in 1851 and 1868—treaties that are legally significant, if never respected in practice. The first treaty established the full extent of the reservation; the second forbade any white (or other) settlement without the express agreement of the Lakota governing council. However, the proposed route of the Dakota Access Pipeline respected none of these treaties: most significantly, it had to cross through sacred lands and Lake Oahe on the Missouri River, which supplies the reservation with potable water. The opposition of Standing Rock residents was justified on the merits of two separate arguments, namely, on environmental and anticolonial grounds.

As for the environment, the pipeline risked polluting potable water resources and local ecosystems on a massive scale. The opponents' fears

---

were justified, and, on the back of an environmental assessment, the courts blocked the pipeline on July 6, 2020. This was the reason why those opposed to the construction of the pipeline—both the First Nations' peoples and ecologists who had been fighting against it since 2014—called themselves "water protectors" and adopted the slogan "Mni Wiconi" (Water Is Life). To affirm that "water is life" is to return to an environmental position that makes the preservation of resources the essential condition of all life. But, as Nick Estes, a researcher and activist of the Lower Brule Sioux tribe, writes, "The protestors called themselves Water Protectors because they weren't simply against a pipeline; they also stood for something greater: the continuation of life on a planet ravaged by capitalism."[16]

In the context of anticolonial action, the Dakota Access Pipeline project can't help but bring to mind the long history of the expropriation of the native peoples of North America. Planned initially to be laid farther north, close to the predominantly white town of Bismarck, the route was abruptly changed to cross over reservation lands. The protestors were critical of this choice, pointing out how it was characteristic of "environmental racism," which makes non-white populations bear an imbalanced risk of ecological catastrophe, reinforcing pre-existing patterns of racial discrimination.[17] The pipeline controversy recalls as well how the land treaties between the "Great Sioux Nation" and the US that were signed in the middle of the nineteenth century have never been respected. Not only would the oil pipeline have had to cross through the reservation, but also under Lake Oahe, a reservoir whose construction flooded Oceti Sakowin lands in the 1960s. Finished in 1962, the reservoir submerged almost all the forests and a large portion of the arable lands of the reservation.[18] Protecting water is the same as defending the conditions of life threatened by the extractivist logic of

---

16 Nick Estes, *Our History Is the Future* (London: Verso, 2019), 15.

17 Razmig Keucheyan, *Nature Is a Battlefield: Toward a Political Ecology*, trans. David Broder (Cambridge: Polity, 2016).

18 Dina Gilio-Whitaker, *As Long as Grass Grows: The Indigenous Fight for Environmental Justice from Colonization to Standing Rock* (Boston: Beacon, 2019), 23.

capitalism, the autonomy of the indigenous peoples, and their right to live on lands seized during colonization.

The Standing Rock movement reveals the role of land in contemporary struggles. Writing about the lands occupied by the DAPL protestors, Estes argues that "[it] didn't matter if this was private property. It was still treaty territory, territory that generations of Lakotas and Dakotas had died defending and lived to care for."[19] Insomuch as it is owned collectively, Standing Rock embodies the history of the political community. It is, at once, the place that assures people of being connected to the conditions of the material reproduction of the group, and it is the space that defines the historical community (by the transmission of the norms of belonging due to the narratives tied to the land). Indigenous territoriality is the opposite of the type of land occupation defined by private property and national sovereignty. National sovereignty is no more than the extension of the economic relations derived from a system of private property to the framework of the political community. In the two cases of sovereignty and property, what is at stake is guaranteeing the possibility of an *exclusive appropriation of land* without the involvement of the proletariat or outsiders. The indigenous territoriality of Standing Rock was quite the opposite: there, the movement aimed to defend *sustainable uses of lands not subject to the laws of property ownership*. This is the critique of capitalist ownership that this struggle announces: neither the land of the ancestors nor the water of life can be subjected to private appropriation.

In fact, there are many examples of indigenous struggles against extractivism: the Chenchu in Andhra Pradesh, the Gwich'in in Alaska, the Bushinengue in French Guiana, the Australian Aborigines demanding the application of the "Land Title Act," or the fight of the Ayllus of the National Council of Ayllus and Markas of Qullasuyu (CONAMAQ) against the exploitation of land in Bolivia. All share the goal of fighting against property relations that set in place the spatial and ecological preconditions for capitalism. Estes concludes his analysis of the Standing Rock movement by emphasizing that because "whether for drinking or

---

19   Estes, *Our History*, 66.

for agriculture, everyone depended on water, and so Mni Wiconi (Water is Life) trumped the sacredness of private property."[20] While opposing the property relations of extractivist capitalism, the Water Protectors are leading a decolonial fight against the expropriation of indigenous lands, an ecological resistance against the destruction of life, and a class struggle against the dispossession of the conditions of subsistence. While not all of its participants champion the cause explicitly, we can say that this struggle is communist because it brings back to life communism's eternal truth, namely, that "familiarity with the oldest of dreams"—the thriving of individuals brought about by the abolition of alienation and misery.[21]

The contemporary face of communism can be found then in what appear, at first, to be its most overused themes: the abolition of private property, historical materialism, the class struggle. But, in order to revivify communism's historical meaning, it is not enough to note how decolonial, ecological, and territorial struggles aspire for a freer world. We must still be able to find an ecological cosmology in today's communism that can turn the preservation of the biosphere into the ecological condition of a communist history of the earth.

"To Escape Naturalism!"

Over the past several decades, the concept of nature has been subjected to heavy critique. The justifiable fear of a naturalization of oppression has led its critics to argue for the abandonment of all naturalist thought. Yet, the current environmental catastrophe asks us to understand the causes and the consequences of what is taking place. The destruction of wilderness, global warming, the mass extinction of fauna, the salinization of water, and the rise in sea level are now globally recognized events.

---

20   Ibid., 26.
21   Ernst Bloch, *Thomas Münzer, théologien de la revolution*, trans. M. de Gandillac (Paris: Les Prairies ordinaires, 2012), 89. [Translator's note: There is no English translation of this work. For German, see Bloch, *Thomas Münzer als Theologe der Revolution* (Berlin: Suhrkamp, 1920).]

In this context, the concept of nature seems newly relevant. Nature has been reappropriated by ecological movements that need a name to mark nonhuman realities facing destruction and in order to think through the power of all that grows by itself. Should naturalism be avoided at all costs, or is it possible to inaugurate a political ecology based on a revitalized concept of nature?

In the history of philosophy, naturalism marks the general idea of how societies claim belonging to the land as well as how there is a continuity between natural phenomena and social facts. A naturalist position most often suggests bringing a practice, discourse, or social representation back to its natural and material substratum. For example, a naturalist explains human behavior through the necessity of an environment adaptation or by the biological function that it fulfills. However, naturalism has borne the brunt of many critiques in the social sciences and in the environmental humanities.

As Stéphane Haber has shown, these critiques reveal the three essential dimensions of the concept of nature. First, a critique inspired by an "anthropological" principle has shown that we cannot infer predetermined social responses from a biological infrastructure. Indeed, social criticism has shown that there has never been any *human nature*, and that external reality (the environment) cannot *determine* human behavior. In other words, there can be no "essential link between human life and nature" that would intervene to explain social phenomena from a natural anchorage.[22] This criticism arises from a program of social emancipation inherited from humanism and Enlightenment philosophy, then repurposed in twentieth-century political philosophy. This critique allows us to avoid the biological and environmental determinism of certain currents of modern Western thought.

Next, a critique from a sociological principle points out that we have never had recourse to nature itself but only to representations of nature, that is, to cultural modalities or techniques for interacting with the environment. This idea has been developed in important ways in

---

22   Stéphane Haber, *Critique de l'antinaturalisme. Études sur Foucault, Butler, Habermas* (Paris: Presses universitaires de France, 2006), 4.

contemporary anthropology. In short, the idea that nature is everywhere the same, always ruled by the same laws, fundamentally material, and that the world's many cultures emerge from it alone has been subjected to a radical deconstruction; in the French-speaking world, Philippe Descola's "anthropology of nature" is perhaps the most famous example of this critique.[23] The ethnographical variations of humanity do not emerge solely through different forms of appropriating nature but, more fundamentally, from ways of identifying a reality that is only rarely thought of in terms of a separation between natural processes and cultural facts. The *naturalist codification of the real* arising from the distinction between universal nature and cultural diversity is only one of the possible ways of identifying the self, the world, and others. For Descola's ecological anthropology, the extension of the concept of nature into nonnatural contexts is the result of a Eurocentric illusion: to the extent that the ontological division upon which it relies does not actually exist, we cannot study societies while looking for the traces of a nature that is ultimately absent.

Finally, concerning critiques about the *normative* dimension of nature, it is best to remember that in anything human, the contingency of practices and the autonomy of collectivities prevent us from deducing what *should be* from what *is*. Nature never provides any ethical rule to routinize practice, nor can it provide a principle from which we could deduce "correct" action. Free will, political choice, and self-organized or imposed collective action are the only bases from which to evaluate social practices.

Due to these legitimate critiques, the concept of nature has today been reinvested with new political and philosophical meaning. In short, it allows us to integrate the processes, landscapes, environments, organic and non-organic entities, and ecosystems, which have suffered under social activity and have had to "pay the price" of a mode of production that does not sustain life's conditions of reproduction. Many ecological movements have focused their critique on the idea of nature

---

23   Philippe Descola, *Beyond Nature and Culture*, trans. Janet Lloyd (Chicago: University of Chicago Press, 2014).

as *what must be protected* against the aggressive incursions of destructive productivism, to wit, the slogan of Notre-Dame-des-Landes: "We're not defending nature, we are nature defending itself."[24] At the same time, environmental ethics has sought to establish a positive conception of the "intrinsic value of nature," so as to show that it is worth defending not only *against* threats weighing against it, but also *for* the internal wealth of its organisms, species, and ecosystems that compose it.[25] It must be seen as worthy of respect in order to serve as the basis for a new ethics that will seek to limit the destructive effects of human practices. Environmental philosophy often champions naturalist positions, that is to say, it considers the existence of "nature" (and not only the "real") as a fact and that knowledge about this fact is possible to obtain. So, while nature has been deconstructed by the social sciences, it has been brought to the forefront again by environmental ethics and ecological movements. On the one hand, we criticize the social effects of a concept of nature deemed determinist, Eurocentric, and normative; on the other hand, we uphold the normativity of an "eternal" nature in order to fight against the ecological harm of a social system that destroys biodiversity.

To escape from the conflict between an ecology stripped of "nature," and a naturalization of the social, I propose an ontology adapted to our era of climate change, one that is taken from an ecological reading of historical materialism.

---

24   Isabelle Frémeaux and Jay Jordan, *We Are "Nature" Defending Itself* (London: Pluto Press, 2021).

25   The "valorization" of nature in an environmental ethics, or the attempt to place in nature an intrinsic value, is part of a movement hoping to recognize the importance of nature as a concept. Speaking of nature allows us to circumscribe human action and its consequences on the environment. See, for example, Holmes Rolston III, "Value in Nature and the Nature of Value," in Robin Attfield and Andrew Belsey, eds., *Philosophy and the Natural Environment* (Cambridge: Cambridge University Press, 1994), 13–30.

Historical Multinaturalism

We can summarize the naturalist aporia in the following way: either we say that nature is always already socialized by human activity, or we can say that nature exists independently from the social.

In the first case, the concept of nature seems useless or reactionary. This is the anti-naturalist position. In short, since nature is always already socialized (it is modeled on practices and represented in discourse), constructing from it any rule to govern practice only allocates to it a "natural" principle that is nothing more than a naturalized social norm. The "naturalness" of heterosexuality is the most obvious example: we naturalize a social fact so as to legitimize the sexual norm that creates it, by setting it up a "natural law." Naturalization plays an ideological role in the legitimation of a power dynamic. Certain uses of the concept of nature are undeniably problematic. However, by denying the use of the concept of nature in order to separate ourselves from these problems, we risk eliminating the forces that the concept seeks to name: the power of life to live and to reproduce. In the second case, nature appears either as what is external to societies (an object to be preserved or dominated), or as the totality in which societies also exist. This is the naturalist position. Nature returns to being a social norm. For example, to want "to preserve the integrity, stability, and beauty of the biotic community" is to set up a certain vision of "nature" as the principle of political organization that can itself be the site of a struggle over the values that we assign to it.[26]

To avoid this conflict between a nature-free ecology and a naturalization of the social, there exists the possibility of *historicizing nature*. We find a first attempt at this in *The German Ideology*:

> For instance, the important question of the relation of man to nature (Bruno [Bauer] goes so far as to speak of "the antitheses in nature and history," as though these were two separate "things" and man did not

---

26 Aldo Leopold, *A Sand County Almanac: And Sketches Here and There* (1949; New York: Ballantine, 1982), 262.

always have before him an historical nature and a natural history), which gave rise to all the "unfathomably lofty works" on "substance" and "self-consciousness," crumbles of itself when we understand that the celebrated "unity of man with nature" has always existed in industry and has existed in varying forms in every era according to the lesser or greater development of industry, and so has the "struggle" of man with nature, right up to the development of his productive forces on a corresponding basis.[27]

The authors criticize with evident irony the transformation of "nature" and "history" into two substances, two realities, "two things," which would exist independently of each other. In reality, nature is historical, and history is natural. Here, it is important to understand that in their production ("industry"), societies are always relating to the "nature" that previous generations have already transformed. The Capitalocene is the prime example of this: the air that we breathe and the ground on which we walk are natural realities that were already modified by previous social activity. In an inverse way, history is "natural" in the sense that all social history begins with life, which would not be able to exist without biotic, climatic, geological, orographic, and other preconditions. Societies as complex as modern capitalist ones cannot reproduce without appropriating an ever-greater part of the earth's biophysical resources (for example, nutrients for eating, sand for concrete, oil for energy, or gold for electronics) without always being in continuous relation with nature.

Natural history and historical natures are the results of a lasting interactive process. The unity of humans and nature is neither a lost *origin* nor an *end* that societies should seek to realize; the unity is constituted by productive activity itself. It is by the production of their material conditions that individuals transform their environment and develop their potential. The rich, Edenic landscapes that the first colonizers "found already there" in North America were the product of a social history of slash-and-burn agriculture, selective

---

27 Engels and Marx, *The German Ideology*, 45–6.

culling, agroforestry, and nomadism. The unity of humans and nature is, then, a continuous historical process of internal transformation led by the more or less conscious modification of the environment. While the idea of human-nature unity is unsatisfactory in some ways, the fact is *all* relations between human and nonhumans, however destructive they may be, bear witness to this fundamental unity. But, since these relations are historical, the form of human-nature unity changes: there are a lot of ways that humans relate to land. But all of these are the results of the changing character of this unity, which takes place in the reproduction of the conditions of existence. There are as many ways of being "one with nature" as there are ways of producing and living in society. So, the fundamental teaching of historical materialism is *the impossibility of naturalizing social relations to nature*: our ways of relating to nonhumans are always determined historically by property relations. But, as the last sentence of the above passage from *The German Ideology* makes clear, in Marx and Engels, there is a lingering ambiguity about productivism and the ideal of the domination of nature.

To the extent that nature-society relations are historical, it's impossible to schematize them with terms as unilateral as *unity* or *struggle*, first, because the struggle is itself a form of their unity, produced by the relation between two antagonistic sides; and, second, because the struggle is permanent. Every society is tied to their environment (as destructive as this relation may be for the environment), and so even in unstable ecosystems there is a constant effort to set down the necessary conditions of social reproduction. Thus, there is no way to retire from nature. In every mode of production, society is dependent on a metabolic regime that is historically determined. Each mode of production defines a certain type of material exchange between societies and their environments. Capitalism's uniqueness is that this exchange is unsustainable. For Marx and Engels, the only way to end the struggle for survival is communism. Liberated from the exploitation of labor, individuals would not be dispossessed of their conditions of subsistence by a particular class. Freed from want by the development of productive forces, they would live in conditions of abundance.[28] The definition of abundance is evidently social. It does not specify any one level of development; it only defines the satisfaction of historically determined social needs. The socialization of nature would effectively guarantee the ecological conditions of a life emancipated from misery and scarcity.

Historical materialism is often caught in a tension between a nature that continues to exist outside of us ("the priority of external nature remains unassailed") and a nature that would be integrally socialized ("[this] nature [that precedes history], today no longer exists anywhere except perhaps on a few Australian coral islands of recent origin.")[29] However, rather than seeing this as an unsustainable paradox, we can rather see here the foundations of a naturalist conception of history that we could call, after Frédéric Monferrand, "historical naturalism."[30]

The central tenet of the historicity of nature and the naturalness of history allows us to bypass the aporias of contemporary critical theory while developing a historical, cultural, and political naturalism. In what follows, I am hoping to formulate a materialist ontology adapted to the Anthropocene, where socialized nature nevertheless remains autonomous. Although the premises for this historical naturalism are found in historical materialism, there is still the need to define the three meanings of the historicity of nature in our time of climate crisis. We cannot avoid a concept of nature because there exist in the real and in life productive and generative powers that do not depend on technological powers.

---

28   Pierre Charbonnier, *Affluence and Freedom: An Environmental History of Political Ideas*, trans. Andrew Brown (Cambridge: Polity, 2021).

29   Engels and Marx, *The German Ideology*, 46.

30   Frédéric Monferrand, *La nature du capital. Politique et ontologie chez le jeune Marx* (Paris: Amsterdam, 2024); Paul Guillibert and Frédéric Monferrand, "Ecology/Ontology: A Contribution to Historical Naturalism," *Dialogue and Universalism* 3 (2018): 245–51.

Nature Is Autonomous

Life has spontaneous generative powers that exist independently of the type of cultural codification in which we couch it. By their isolated and joint action, organisms and ecosystems produce material effects. Interactions between living entities transform the environment, which, in turn, conditions the forms of life that can develop there. These interrelations produce an *environment*, which is the result of reciprocal actions of the organisms in each biotope. This dynamic definition of ecosystems accords an important place to their generative power, or to their capacity to fix in place, by their interactions, the norms of possible action in any specific environment. Let us consider the effects of mycorrhiza, the network of roots and fungi that provides the necessary conditions for the growth of certain tree species, or the millions of years necessary for the decomposition of organic material to make fossil fuels. Nature demonstrates its unending reproductive and generative power. Donna Haraway recently proposed to replace the concept of "self-production" with that of "sympoiesis," which speaks of the coproduction of the environment through species that interact rather than defining the environment as the autonomous activity of isolated organisms.[31] Environments are always, then, "multispecific worlds," composed of the actions of different life forms.[32] The specifics of Haraway's claim are instructive, but she bases her argument on a common idea about the nature of the real: there are powers of productivity that incite life independent of our representations of them. These processes are usually grouped under the name "natural history," but it would be better to think of them as part of *an autonomous history of nature*. In sum, a conversion is performed on naturalism similar to the one to which Marx and Engels subjected Ludwig Feuerbach's materialism: nature is not only given, it is also coproduced; life is not only affected by external conditions but is also capable of transforming the environment by interspecific productivity.

---

31 Donna Haraway, *Staying with the Trouble: Making Kin in the Chthulucene* (Durham, NC: Duke University Press, 2016), 33.
32 Ibid., 6.

"Nature" is the name most often given to this host of forces and potentialities in the history of European thought. Along with the anti-naturalists, we acknowledge that "nature" is only ever one specific culture's codification of the real, but that it can be allowed, under certain conditions, to refer to nonhuman realities and to authorize translations consistent with other cultural codifications. The concept of nature allows us to name nonhuman, non-technological generative powers. Moreover, the insistence of repeating the term "nonhuman" in contemporary environmental literature bears witness to the need of a concept to name these realities that are not produced by societies, a genre of realities that we are already used to calling by the name "nature." The result is the emergence of a practical naturalism in which autonomous nature is self-generating.

Autonomy is the power of action that active beings have within the environment in which they are evolving and whose modification they help effectuate through their shared actions. Because environments are the results of the specific coevolution of species (sympoiesis), it would be more meaningful to speak of the "symbionomia of natures" rather than the autonomy of nature. Heteronomy is, then, a limitation of the deployment of the nature of a being or an ecosystem by the implementation of rules and norms more in keeping with the nature of other beings. With this in mind, to say that nature has a heteronomous history is to insist on the scope of constraints, limitations, orientations, perturbations, and destructions that societies could impose on the unfurling of its logic.

Nature Is Historical

This autonomous power of the procreation of the real (or "symbionomia") emerges within culturally and historically determined conditions, which is to say, conditions that are informed by a heteronomous social history. Nature has a social history in the sense that it is transformed by human activities, which themselves are informed by cosmologies that "encode" the real. Think of the transformation of nature in the American

West during colonialism, or at the heights of industrial capitalism.[33] We can see that the autonomous history of nature is heavily modified by the *heteronomous history of nature*, which is its social and cultural history. The conditions of the emergence of nature are always culturally situated. Talking about the social history of nature is the same as citing the coeval nature of human practices and their objective material conditions. The ravaged forests of Oregon where matsutake mushrooms flourish is one example. As Anna Tsing shows in *The Mushroom at the End of the World*, it's in abandoned clear-cut forests that these coveted mushrooms grow. For mushrooms to be viable in this environment, there has to be both an autonomous history (the effects of mycorrhiza) and a heteronomous or social history of nature (the clear-cutting of trees after which the ecosystem is abandoned). Tsing proposes a name for this autonomous nature that surges forth from the ruins of capitalism and the destruction of the world's ecosystems. She calls it "third nature." [34] This concept allows us to identify the historical result of the symbioses in operation among the nonhuman agents of advanced anthropological transformation. Old species have returned to ecosystems that we would have assumed degraded by extractivism past the point of no return, just as new species have settled there as well. There are different types of natural beings that are determined by the relations they hold with capitalist history: wild and free nature, exploited nature that is transformed by capital, and nature that is rewilded by the generative power of its species.

Each time ecosystems are changed or abandoned, new interactions emerge, producing new environments, which can then disturb the accumulation of capital—for example, the type of amaranth that has become resistant to Roundup, the Monsanto herbicide designed to kill all plants except those genetically modified to resist it. This "super-bad weed" will be found henceforth in a highly anthropized, degraded environment,

---

33   William Cronon, *Nature's Metropolis: Chicago and the Great West* (New York: Norton, 1991).

34   Anna Lowenhaupt Tsing, *The Mushroom at the End of the World* (Princeton, NJ: Princeton University Press, 2015).

and yet it will resist this degradation.[35] Nature has an autonomous history and a social history. The materialist conception of the historicity of nature explains at once the destructive force of socialization (the Capitalocene) and its autonomy (sympoiesis).

Nature Is Multiple

Because sympoiesis is the interactive capacity of different organisms and species to be productive, its history is necessarily multiple. There is not one history of nature but *many* "natural histories."[36] These natural histories are the always partial and incomplete product of a power of self-generation that is found within nonhuman environments and human societies. In this way, this materialist history of nature is a "multinaturalism." It admits that nonhuman generative capacity is always relative to the natural environments and the history of societies that transformed it materially and informed it symbolically. I use the term "nature" in the singular to mean an ontological generative power that never exists except in singular manifestations, which is to say, in real historical natures. These historical natures mark human and nonhuman realities to which the self-generating power of procreation is subjected. In other words, "nature" does not refer to a space of a collection of objects; rather, the word attempts to mark off a causal power that is present only in specific "natures." It is for this reason that this ontology is a *multinaturalism*. The multinaturalism that I propose is, then, very different from the "multinatural perspectivism" set forth by the anthropologist Eduardo Viveiros de Castro, who seeks to understand the position of the shaman, theorizing that differences in the intensities of human and animal worlds is generated from within each living being.[37] From this point of view, all life

---

35   Léna Balaud and Antoine Chopot, *Nous ne sommes pas seuls. Politiques des soulèvements terrestres* (Paris: Seuil, 2021).

36   Jason W. Moore, *Capitalism in the Web of Life: Ecology and the Accumulation of Capital* (London: Verso, 2015).

37   Eduardo Viveiros de Castro, *Cannibal Metaphysics*, trans. Peter Skafish (Minneapolis: University of Minnesota Press, 2014), 60.

forms have their way of constituting an objective world, a "nature," relative to their subjective constitution. In my use of the term "multinaturalism," I aim instead to include the historicity of natural beings, which is to say, the relations between society and naturalism that dictate the transformation of all historical entities. Simply put, I am championing a historical multinaturalism, a cosmology for communism in the Anthropocene.

2

Capital Does Nothing in Vain: The Historical Naturalism of Karl Marx

Moreover, nature has evolved under the effects of constant nuclear radia-
tion. The spectrum of living species had diminished, and, after a short
period of mutations when baroque and spectacular apparitions could be
seen, sterility had reigned, and the planet had returned to an essentially
vegetal state. Contrary to scholars' predictions, which as usual were
contradicted by chance, spiders and arachnids in general hadn't filled the
spaces opened up by the decline of the animals. For 81 decades and then
some, flies had looked like they would be a dominant species, and, then, in
turn, they had been extinguished without leaving any kin. Several survi-
vors in the taiga with feathers or fur eked out a living, but their numbers
were negligible, and, in short, the Gramma Udgul was one of the last
earthly creatures endowed with a brain and several appendages. If she had
been 1,977 years younger, maybe she would have set out to start, on a
small scale, a Third Soviet Union, but now age played its evil stifling role
and she had no longer had the strength.

—Antoine Volodine, *Radiant Terminus*, trans. Jeffrey Zuckerman

The problem of naming is not strictly a philosophical concern. We first
have to find languages adapted to the natural worlds we want to save
before we can set in motion plans to save them. It goes without saying

that different cosmologies—ways of identifying the world, the self, and others—initiate different ways of relating to the environment. But these cultures of nature do not exist in isolation; they are not completely autonomous from other spheres of the social world. As the philosopher of science Carolyn Merchant has said, the invention of mechanical and passive nature, compacted into an object under the gaze of masculine desire, coincides with the emergence of early modern capitalist extractivist practices. Images are not just a thoughtless representation of nature, but they mobilize norms that authorize or implicitly forbid certain practices. To the extent that representations must be matched to practices to claim to justify them, cosmologies evolve as well in relation to the history of other spheres of social reality. There are always differences and tensions, to wit, contradictions between usage patterns and the symbolic forms that legitimize them.[1] Individuals seek to embody social norms, which they achieve and modify at the same time. In short, the material relations of nature are never the simple expression of an ontology, as is said too often in ecological literature and contemporary anthropology. Of course, that does not mean that a transformation of the ways of identifying the world is without importance for an ecological revolution but, rather, that this transformation cannot be reduced to an ontological negotiation concerning the distribution of the sensible.

In this chapter, I will develop a materialist conception of the ecological history of societies. By materiality, I mean the objective interdependencies of life (for instance, the circulation of matter and energy), social relations, and their metabolism. Societies actualize human potential by developing more substantial material relations (and in greater number) with nonhuman worlds. But social activities never develop solely from the naturalness already found there; they also inherit the means and objects of labor from previous social activity.[2] Nature is socialized. So, in

---

1 Carolyn Merchant, *The Death of Nature: Women, Ecology, and the Scientific Revolution* (New York: Harper & Row, 1980).

2 The activities of human production develop from nature (that which has not been transformed by human activity) and from the products of prior human activity. For example, to refine oil, it first has to be extracted from the ground: raw petroleum is at once natural and the product of prior human activity. In this case, *naturalness* is

fact, social formations belong to a nature that preexists them, but in which they evolve, while interacting with nature on the basis of established property relations.

It is reductive to imagine that the modern dualism that sets society against nature is the root cause of the destruction of nature. The idea of a discontinuity between natural phenomena and cultural processes can be understood in many ways and can lead to very different practices. Yet, based on some of Marx's writing, we can reinscribe the epistemological discontinuity of dualism into the ecological history of capitalist societies. Nevertheless, the polarities of labor and land, humanity and nature, and subject and object register no longer in our minds as the dualist presuppositions of a philosophy of production, but as the historical result of private appropriation in class-based societies. Because, for Marx, property relations modify the ways we relate to nature, and they produce specific historical trajectories.

Property Relations and Ways of Relating to Nature

Within the ontological turn in the social sciences, an entire literature has arisen regarding the ecological effects of property and the strategic role of the "commons."[3] Rather than privileging the study of cosmologies, this social-scientific literature pays special attention to the ways that nature is appropriated within the environmental history of societies. To be sure, the ways that societies appropriate their environment do condition their relation to nature more than the forms through which these societies represent their environment. Yet, we already find traces of this materialist history of the environment in the *Grundrisse*, the notebooks of 1857 to 1858 that were Marx's first systematic attempts to draft

---

the effect, the specific object-product, that is to say, the results of an autonomous power of generation that we call "nature." I use the term "object" and "objective" for their difference from "subject," and so that which is affected by action (or is the result of action) and *not* as a subject, or that which affects through action.

3   Frédéric Graber and Fabien Locher, eds., *Posséder la nature. Environnement et propriété dans l'histoire* (Paris: Amsterdam, 2018).

Capital.[4] These notebooks include an otherwise-unpublished historical chapter where Marx attempts to study property relations in noncapitalist communitarian societies.

The chapter "Pre-capitalist Economic Formations" has led historians and anthropologists toward a materialist study of social relations in agrarian societies.[5] For example, Eric Hobsbawm cites the chapter to support his claim that in historical materialism,

> [the] interaction between man and nature is, and produces, social evolution. Taking from nature, or determining the use of some bit of nature (including one's own body) can be, and indeed is in common parlance, seen as an appropriation, which is therefore originally merely an aspect of labor.[6]

In this chapter on precapitalist societies, the historicism of the young Marx begins to develop. The four forms of non-capitalist communities that he studies (primitive, Asian, Greco-Roman, German) are presented in succession, as if they indicated the trajectory of humanity from its origins up till its most "developed" forms on the brink of capitalism. And yet, Marx is attentive to the geography of modes of production and the multiplicity of possible futures for each society. This is the reason we can read it as a "multilinear schema" of history where communities evolve according to the modes of appropriation of nature and labor.[7] Within

---

4   [Translator's note: The notebooks that comprise the *Grundrisse* were misplaced then rediscovered in the twentieth century and published for the first time in German in 1939 and in English in 1973. This "historical chapter" would appear neither in *A Contribution to the Critique of Political Economy* (1859) nor in *Capital* (1867, 1885, 1894).]

5   In addition to the historian Eric Hobsbawm (1917–2012), who introduced this text in English in a stand-alone edition in 1964, there is also the work of Robert Brenner, Ellen Meiksins Wood, and Maurice Godelier. See Karl Marx, *Pre-capitalist Economic Formations*, trans. Jack Cohen, ed. Eric Hobsbawm (London: Lawrence & Wishart, 1964).

6   Eric Hobsbawm, introduction to Marx, *Pre-capitalist Economic Formations*, 9–66 (12).

7   Maurice Godelier, preface to Karl Marx, Friedrich Engels, and Vladimir Lenin, *Sur les sociétés précapitalistes. Textes choisis de Marx, Engels, Lénine*, ed. Centre

this rubric, the appearance of the category of the Asian agrarian community is ambivalent. It manifests simultaneously the Eurocentrism of the author, who collapses non-European societies of extremely different types (India, Mexico, Romania, Peru) into a homogenous category ("Asian"), and the desire to introduce a mode of production that escapes the linear and mechanical succession of historical stages. It is important to note that Marx's primitive communes are "distillations" or abstract "types" that make it possible to think through the historical emergence of class societies and, in short, the relations of capitalist production.[8] Unlike *Capital*, whose historical chapters study the passage between different forms of private property, this part of the *Grundrisse* studies capital's emergence in societies founded on communal property. Beyond the primitive collectivity that he considers universal, Marx identifies three archaic agrarian communes founded on collective property, each different in how it approaches the distribution of land and the accumulation of transferable securities.

The first category, the Asian agrarian community, is defined as a "natural community," which is to say, a society founded on family relations in which pastoralism is practiced. This snapshot covers a large variety of societies that are all different geographically, culturally, and historically. Marx sees it simultaneously in ancient Indian societies, Amerindian societies like Mexico and pre-Inca Peru, and in European societies like Romania. In this case, the communal organization of society and collective labor precedes communal property. To speak of this in more contemporary terms, labor organization and the access to land are regulated by kinship. In this scenario, a multitude of little communes exist side by side. In these societies, "[the] earth is the great laboratory, the arsenal which provides both the means of labor and the materials of labor, and also the location, the *basis* of the community."[9] Communal possession

---

d'études et de recherches marxistes (Paris: Éditions sociales, 1970), 16. [Translator's note: This book was recently re-edited, with a preface and introduction by Godelier, as well as a note from the publishers. See Godelier, preface to Marx, Engels, and Lenin, *Sur les sociétés précapitalistes*, rev. ed. (Paris: Éditions sociales, 2022), 7–24.]

8   Ibid., 52.
9   Marx, *Pre-capitalist Economic Formations*, 69.

by the family or the village established the land at the heart of social and natural reproduction. Each person is considered to be a member of the collectivity and a landowner. Meanwhile, little by little, the dispersion of communities and the development of large-scale infrastructure projects (most importantly, water-management projects) leads to the appearance of large institutions and "despotic" centralizing states, which own the land and parcel it out based on kinship precedent to the village communities that use it collectively. We could say that the centralized institution becomes a sort of "bare owner," and that the local communities are only "usufructuaries." At the same time, no one owns anything individually because the land belongs to the governing institutions of the collectivity. Individuals only have the right to use the land for brief periods. There is no separation between land and community: the one is the spatial existence of the other. This also means that the village appears like an extension of the field. In these various historical forms, we find quite often a structural element: the "collective force of the workers" (productive and reproductive) contributes more to village organization than communal property.[10]

Then, in the Greco-Roman agrarian commune, the second form that Marx proposes, cultivated fields are village property. This commune is characterized by an inversion in the relation between the village and the countryside: "The cultivated field here appears as a *territorium* belonging to the town; not the village as mere accessory to the land."[11] Two forms of property are simultaneously apparent: the communal property of the Roman state, *ager publicus*, and private property. Unlike in the first form, the collective labor organization is at once less present and less constraining. Yet, all societies of this type (they are quite varied) tend toward hostilities. The subsistence of the state and the community depend on the ability to gain agricultural land to feed the urban centers. The population is concentrated in towns, small-scale agriculture is geared toward immediate consumption, and manufacturing is only an

---

10   Karl Marx, *Grundrisse*, trans. Martin Nicolaus (London: Penguin, 1973), 569.
11   Ibid., 474.

ancillary activity. The durability of this form of community is based on the maintenance of equality among the peasants whose lives are defined by just getting by. Here, then, a part of the land is communal because it belongs directly to the community through the mediation of individuals, who can only access the property in their guise as citizens. According to Marx, in this form, "it is genuinely the common property of the individual owners."[12] The individual does not work to reproduce the collectivity but to reproduce themself as a member of the community.

Marx spends less time considering the German agrarian commune, the third form. Here, the commune is tantamount to an organization of the members of a clan who live separately in the forest or countryside. It's not a "unity-in-itself" but a "coming together." The commune effectively acts as one only in its assemblies. Families are autonomous units that join forces only when called to do so. Communal property is the simple "complement to individual property."[13]

The anthropological typecasting of these forms presents a problem that is beyond the scope of this book to address. Nevertheless, the way that Marx thinks through the relations of natural materiality is important, and each of these agrarian communes possesses a unique mode of relating to nature. The uses of the land are determined by labor methods but also by property relations and ways of occupying territory. This last aspect is essential for the formulation of an ecological communism. The political geography of societies is expressed by the various relations between the urban and the rural. The Asian agrarian communes are defined by the indissoluble unity of the town and the countryside (especially between the artisan class and agriculture), the Greco-Roman commune is defined by the "ruralization of the town," and the German commune is defined by the "urbanization of the countryside."[14] The tendency of crossing over the division of the town and the countryside will lead to the functional separation of agrarian and industrial production in capitalism. Marx's originality here consists in defining societies

---

12   Marx, *Pre-capitalist Economic Formations*, 80.
13   Ibid., 486.
14   Ibid., 484.

by their relations to the land and to territory. These are expressed in how nature is appropriated and how the environment is divided into units of labor. It's this territoriality of the relations of production that makes the study of precapitalist societies essential for the ecological rereading of historical materialism. To be sure, in the *Grundrisse*, the premises of territorial ecology appear: a non-perturbed metabolism between societies and nature depends on the modes of access to the land, control of the land, and its usage.

In sum, these societies share three features. First, the goal of an economy is the production of goods adapted to social needs and not the accumulation of exchange values. These communal agrarian societies strive for "the *reproduction of the individual* within the specific relations to the commune in which [the individual] is its basis."[15] The reproduction of the individual is at once the individual's subsistence as a living being and the repetition of the type of relations that the individual has with the community. In these contexts, the individual is first a member of a group; society is not thought of as a sum of members who preexist society. The individual is defined first by affiliations. The underdevelopment of individuality must be recognized here, as well as the often-conservative character of communitarian forms of organization. Second, land and resources would seem to be the "natural conditions of production [the producer's existence]," or what is presupposed to exist before all activity, without which human existence is not possible.[16] Third, the modes of relating to nature are determined by forms of land appropriation, the means of production, and the environmental division of social labor. What fundamentally unites these three types of the agrarian commune is that collective property guarantees a form of unity with the land, which private property puts to an end:

> It is not the *unity* of living and active humanity with the natural, inorganic conditions of their metabolic exchange with nature, and hence their appropriation of nature, which requires explanation or is the

15   Ibid., 485.
16   Ibid., 489.

result of a historic process, but rather the *separation* between these inorganic conditions of human existence and this active existence, a separation which is completely posited only in the relation of wage labor and capital.[17]

Here, a gloss is necessary for the terms "metabolic exchange" (*Stoffwechsel*) and "ecology." Marx never uses the word "ecology," which was invented the year before the publication of *Capital*, in 1866, by the German physiologist Ernst Haeckel, whose work Marx knew.[18] In keeping with a nineteenth-century trend, he preferred the concept of "metabolism," which seemed to him better suited for thinking through the continuous interactions between an organism and its environment. Haeckel himself was aware of the limits of physiology as a means to think through the relations between the individual and the environment, seeing as how it focuses on the interactions between organs inside a single organism.[19] The concept of metabolism, which Marx would later find in the scientific agronomy of Justus von Liebig in the middle of the 1860s, allowed him to think through "the economy of nature as a whole."[20] In 1857–58, when he wrote the *Grundrisse*, Marx had not yet read Liebig's ecological theory of metabolism; rather, he borrowed this non-ecological concept from German idealism and, especially, from the philosopher Schelling.[21] Later, after reading Liebig's book on agronomy, he identified the material exchanges between organic and inorganic substances without which life would be impossible. This allowed Marx to study the interactions between an organism and its environment through the intermediary of the processes of

---

17   Ibid.

18   Kohei Saito, *Karl Marx's Ecosocialism: Capital, Nature, and the Unfinished Critique of Political Economy* (New York: Monthly Review, 2017), 276.

19   Ernst Haeckel, *Generelle Morphologie der Organismen* (Berlin: Georg Reimer, 1866), 287.

20   Saito, *Karl Marx's Ecosocialism*, 276.

21   Hilmar Westholm, *Stoffwechsel des Menschen mit der Natur. Zu einem qualitativen Naturbegriff von Schelling und von Marx* (Oldenburg: Bibliotheks- und Informationssystem der Universität Oldenburg, 1986).

production, consumption, and digestion.[22] These three functions tie together an organism and its environment on the level of individual life forms, species, and societies. Marx used this concept to name natural interactions, to name exchanges between society and nature, or sometimes to name economic relations themselves, inasmuch as they can be represented as material flux. The fact that the concept is employed at once in physiology, chemistry, and political economy makes it especially interesting. If, today, we can speak of Marx's "ecology" in spite of him never using the term, it's because the concept of metabolism approaches how the word is used today: both serve as a means to articulate a theory of the continuous interactions between life and the environment in a dynamic and non-static totality of open processes.

In the end, Marx distinguished between two antagonistic modes of relating to nature, according to which property relations (collective or private) produce a healthy metabolism between society and the environment, or an unhealthy one. The first is "unity" between activity in general and the "natural, inorganic conditions" of human life; this is a socio-ecological metabolism.[23] The second is the separation of humans and land. This mode disturbs the material exchanges thanks to which life can develop and realize its potential. In the context of Marx's writing on pre-capitalist forms of production, this opposition serves to mark the difference between classless societies (where private property is absent or underdeveloped) and class-based societies, including capitalism.

Communism of Belonging in Classless Societies

In the passage above, defining the environment through the "*inorganic* conditions of human existence" implies that the activity of *living* humans is, by contrast, their *organic* condition. Thus, Marx does not separate

---

22 Saito, *Karl Marx's Ecosocialism*, 69.
23 Marx, *Grundrisse*, 489.

human societies from nature, but, *within the natural totality itself*, he distinguishes between the "organic" and "inorganic" body of human beings. The first represents the body itself as a natural force capable of acting, transforming, and being affected by its environment, while the second expresses the external conditions of the activity that the subject finds already there, the presuppositions of the subject's activity. The concept of the "inorganic *body*" returns, then, to the essential, subjective, and objective duality of the human body: "These *natural conditions of existence*, to which he relates as to his own inorganic body, are themselves double: (1) of a subjective and (2) of an objective nature."[24] A reading that is too facile and dualistic could leave the reader with the impression that the human body is the subject of action and the environment, its object. However, Marx insists on the objective dimension of human action, which is in a permanent relationship with these inorganic conditions, and on the subjective dimension of the environment. Human life is possible only to the extent that it's in relation with objects that it appropriates, and thanks to which it continues. From this point of view, the human condition is objectively natural: we are objects alongside and acting together with other objects. But, at the same time, the "natural conditions of its existence" are equally subjective, to the extent that the human "relates to a specific nature (say, here, still earth, land, soil) as his own inorganic being, as a condition of his production and reproduction."[25] To the extent that the individual sees in nature the condition of their existence, the individual is given to see nature as the body's inorganic part (providing food, sources of heat, and plants that make textiles for clothes). This implies that nature is a part of the individual, even a part of subjectivity.

In sum, to claim that the environment is inorganic reveals our human hubris: firewood (inorganic) that we use for heat was first a living tree (organic) before being harvested, just as a human corpse is also part of inorganic nature that can replenish living organic nature (worms, mushrooms, bacteria). The distinction between the organic and the inorganic

---

24 Ibid., 490.
25 Ibid.

is determined by humankind's material needs. This "perspectivism" is found in Marx's *Economic and Philosophic Manuscripts of 1844*:[26]

> The sun is the *object* of the plant—an indispensable object to it, confirming its life—just as the plant is an object of the sun, being an *expression* of the life-awakening power of the sun, of the sun's *objective* essential power.
>
> A being which does not have its nature outside itself is not a *natural* being, and plays no part in the system of nature.[27]

Natural beings have interdependent objective relations: plants cannot exist without sunlight, which jump-starts photosynthesis, and yet, at the same time, solar energy is materialized, or made into an object in the plant. From the plant's point of view, the sun is an object that gives it energy. From the point of view of the sun, plants are the objective realization of its activity. The idea of the human inorganic body is based on the fact that natural beings exist in a system of needs and interdependence that defines their nature. The nature (essence) of each natural being is defined by the collection of its relations with other natural beings.

The subjective and the objective no longer mark the division of the individual from nature. Just as the human subject is the object of nature, so too the environment appears as a subject inasmuch as it belongs fundamentally to the forces that make it possible for human life to continue. This use of the concept of "body" is wholly original. It does not imply a separation of a limit between the self and the world, but it inscribes, rather, human action in a material continuity with the land, itself understood as a body. The body is no longer the envelope of an

---

26   Judith Butler, "The Inorganic Body in the Early Marx: A Limit-Concept of Anthropocentrism," *Radical Philosophy* 2, no. 6 (Winter 2019): 3–17, 14. Butler uses the terms "perspectival theory" and "perspectival variation."

27   Karl Marx, *Economic and Philosophic Manuscripts of 1844*, trans. Martin Milligan (Moscow: Progress Publishers, 1977), 145. A note on this edition specifies that the English translations of the Progress Publishers' edition are taken from *Collected Works*. See Karl Marx and Friedrich Engels, *Collected Works*, vol. 3, trans. Martin Milligan (London: Lawrence & Wishart, 1959).

individuation but the subjective and objective substratum of life in general.

The distinction between organic and inorganic bodies returns us to Marx's naturalism, or the idea that all natural beings are defined by the type of relation they hold with objective others without whom they cannot exist. Here, it must be said that this naturalism is neither a dualism of substance—the existence of two realities that would exist in fundamental separation—nor a monism incapable of thinking through the discontinuities between the organic and inorganic in a natural totality constituted by objective interactions. The basis of this naturalist ontology is precisely the system of the reciprocal needs of natural beings being differentiated by their ability to affect and be affected. In the first situation of "the *unity* of living and active humanity with the natural, inorganic conditions," human beings relate to the land as though it were a part of themselves (a subjective dimension of the environment) because they know that they belong to the natural totality (the objective dimension of human life).[28]

But this ontological naturalism is determined by the history of property relations. In effect, the joint appearance of the objective character of the human and the subjective dimension of the nonhuman is possible only when land is held as communal property. It's only because the individual is a "natural member of a human community" that the individual can be seen as a part of nature, and that the land appears as an essential part of the individual's subjectivity.[29] Marx inventively compares land held as collective property with linguistic appropriation:

> As regards the individual, it is clear e.g. that he relates even to language itself *as his own* only as a natural member of a human community. Language as the product of an individual is an impossibility. But the same holds true for property.[30]

---

28 Marx, *Grundrisse*, 489.
29 Ibid.
30 Ibid.

Language exists because it is appropriated by the individuals who speak it and enrich it with their unique ways of speaking. The individual's appropriation of language is the condition of its social existence. Inversely, for an individual to say that a language is "his" or "hers," it must have already been learned: the individual has appropriated a set of language practices that can be subsequently put into action. The individual's existence as a "person who speaks this language" is relative to the social existence of a language open to appropriation by anyone at all. The individual can then define their linguistic identity precisely because this language is that of the community to which the individual belongs. The relation to the self through language is a relation to the community that speaks that language. The analogy that Marx proposes is the following: just as an individual defines language as belonging to the self because language is part of the community to which the individual belongs, so too the individual can define land as their own because it belongs collectively to the community in which the individual is a member. Claiming a language to be our "own" presupposes belonging to a community defined by this language. Relating to the land as though it were *one's own*, or a constitutive element of subjectivity, presupposes belonging to a social group defined by this belonging to the land. It's as a member of a group whose identity is defined by the collective appropriation of a territory that the individual can possess land as though it were one's own. It's for this reason that Marx writes that the individual, as a member of an agrarian community,

> relates to a specific nature (say, here, still earth, land, soil) as his own inorganic being, as a condition of his production and reproduction. As a natural member of the community he participates in the communal property, and has a particular part of it as his possession . . . His *property*, i.e. the relation to the natural presuppositions of his production as belonging to him, as *his*, is mediated by his being himself the natural member of a community.[31]

---

31   Ibid.

Territory is that part of nature that furnishes the natural conditions for the reproduction of the group and guarantees its social existence.[32] For the individual, land is now like a part of the self, since land is the condition of individual existence that all group members collectively possess. Through the mediation of group property, the individual relates to nature like an objective condition of its existence, like a part of the self. Property is, then, defined as "the relation to the natural presuppositions of [the individual's] production as belonging to [oneself]," or, the totality of nonhuman realities that humans find already in existence as the conditions of subsistence.[33] People "relate[s] to a specific nature," or a part of the environment that a group accesses to satisfy their specific needs.[34] "The unity of living and active humanity with the natural, inorganic conditions of their metabolic exchange with nature" is therefore guaranteed by communal property.[35] But there is a problem. Since humans live within environments, how can we explain the "separation" between societies and natures? The idea of separation from nature is, by definition, impossible since it leads to the end of all human life. So do the tropes of unity and separation create clichéd notions of classless societies "in harmony" with nature, and class-based societies that destroy their environment?

Organic and Inorganic Bodies in Class-Based Societies

For Marx, because property relations guarantee the real unity of humans with nature, capital, as a social relation, brings about their separation. Marx claims not that a capitalist mode of production is the only one that separates "living and active humanity" from the "inorganic conditions of existence," but that, in contrast to all others, a capitalist mode of production produces a "separation which is completely posited only in the

---

32   Maurice Godelier, "L'appropriation de la nature. Territoire et propriété dans quelques formes de société précapitalistes," *La Pensée* 198 (1978): 7–50.

33   Marx, *Grundrisse*, 490.

34   Ibid.

35   Ibid., 489.

relation of wage labour and capital."[36] The unity of the organic and inorganic in the natural body is riven into two distinct elements, and this "historical process was the divorce" of land and labor consecrated by primitive accumulation.[37] The beginning of private property relations, which authorize the monopolization of community lands, prevents individuals from accessing their means of subsistence. Natural separation is the effect of a dissolution of group relations from territory, the very territory thanks to which individuals gained free access to the land insomuch as the land belonged collectively to their community.

Marx tries to explain the transformation of classless societies into class-based ones. He develops here an element that his later thinking on "so-called primitive accumulation" will not deal with.[38] The birth of capital does not uniquely presuppose the existence of a market of "free" laborers, or ones separated from their means of production. Capital rears its head only after the dissolution of community ties, or the separation of individuals from the land that provides their means of subsistence. In other words, the chapter of *Capital* on primitive accumulation in Great Britain, because it deals only with the transformation from feudal private property to private capitalist property, does not touch upon the destruction of the natural community in classless societies. Yet, in feudal Europe, the separation had already been largely carried out. Only the study of societies founded on communal property can reveal the secondary presupposition of capital, which is the separation of individuals from their natural conditions of existence. The result of this dispossession is double. First, in terms of the owners of their own labor, individuals are subjected to capital's power. Second, they are now merely subjects and, as such, stripped of all objectivity:

> These are, now, on one side, historic presuppositions needed before the
> worker can be found as a free worker, as objectless, purely subjective

---

36   Ibid.
37   Ibid., 503.
38   Karl Marx, *Capital: A Critique of Political Economy*, trans. Ben Fowkes (Harmondsworth: Penguin, 1976), 9.

labour capacity confronting the objective conditions of production as his not-property, as alien property, as value-for-itself, as capital.[39]

The separation of producers from their means of subsistence corresponds to a "historical/absolute divorce" between the human and nonhuman. From an anthropological point of view, it corresponds to the "loss of objectivity." This theme is essential to the *Economic and Philosophic Manuscripts of 1844*, and it's discussed here in the specific context of the transition to capitalism and the appearance of private ownership of the natural conditions of labor. So, to what can we attribute this loss of objectivity?

According to Franck Fischbach, this loss is attributable to the loss of *objects* with which the individual can assure self-reproduction, in other words, the satisfaction of the individual's needs and the growth of the person's individual power.[40] It also marks the loss of the *means of labor*, thanks to which the individual can produce objects, of which, as well, the individual is dispossessed in wage labor. But the material loss of the means of subsistence is also a loss of *objectivity in general*. To the extent that human subjects are objective beings, or fully fledged members of the natural totality without which they cannot exist, and to the extent that they bring about their essential objectivity through labor, the separation from the land corresponds to a loss of their objective being. Consequently, subjects appear as "purely subjective labour capacity," and nature appears as pure objectivity estranged from these subjects.[41] The birth of class-based societies presupposes, then, a *material* separation of humans and nature, and it produces *the idea* of a separable nature. Alienation, or the loss of objectivity, as an expression of a sundered totality, is the result of a dispossession of land that strips from humanity our relation to our intrinsic naturalness, and it condemns nature to being only a passive external environment. Rather than being process-based, the separation

---

39 Marx, *Grundrisse*, 498.

40 Franck Fischbach, introduction to Karl Marx, *Manuscrits économico-philosophiques de 1844*, trans. Franck Fischbach (Paris: Vrin, 2007), 31.

41 Marx, *Grundrisse*, 498.

is, then, rigidly conceptualized as the subjectivity of the human body and the objectivity of nature's body. Subjects, in turn, appear as false subjects stripped of all objectivity, and objects appear as false objects deprived of the subjectivity that allows them to produce and reproduce.

Contrary to popular belief, the dualism of societies and nature does not appear in Marx as a presupposition of an ontology of production; rather, it appears as the historical result of the separation initiated by the private appropriation of the objective conditions of human life.[42] Once again, in class-based societies, the distinction of subjective and objective is not the same as the distinction between culture and nature, or the individual and the world. To the contrary, nature appears as the dynamic unity of matter (raw materials) in flux and exchange where the body encompasses the organic human and the inorganic nonhuman. The initial divorce is set in stone in the history of wage labor. While the *Economic and Philosophic Manuscripts of 1844* takes wage labor in European societies as its analytical subject and discovers there the fundamental separation of labor from the conditions of production, "Pre-capitalist Economic Formations" takes as its beginning point the historical divorce of land and community in classless societies in order to show how this separation prepares the earth to be exploited by the individual in wage labor. Where the *Economic and Philosophic Manuscripts of 1844* were studying alienation from the standpoint of wage labor, Marx's writing in 1857 and 1858 propose something else, namely, a global genealogy of the historical emergence of class-based societies.

However, in the *Grundrisse*, the idea of an ecological history of societies is sometimes still contradicted by a historicism that presents social evolution as an emancipatory rupture with nature. The *Grundrisse* is still marked by the unilinear evolutionism from which Marx was breaking. His attachment to primitive teleology is clearly in evidence in the relation that he establishes between nature and history:

---

42 See Philippe Descola, *Beyond Nature and Culture*, trans. Janet Lloyd (Chicago: University of Chicago Press, 2014).

But human beings become individuals only through the process of history. He appears originally as a *species-being* (*Gattungswesen*), *clan being, herd animal*—although in no way whatever as a ζῷον πολιτικόν (*zoon politikon*) in the political sense. Exchange itself is a chief means of this individuation (*Vereinzelung*). It makes the herd-like existence superfluous and dissolves it.[43]

Homogeneity and herd sociability are *prehistoric* modes of existence for community members who are not yet individuated. The historical process is akin to a rupture with origins, where the human being is only a "herd animal." Historicity begins with individuation, which is the precondition for political action or debate in the Aristotelian sense. It's as though we had a natural origin from which we were deracinated by history. Here, we can see the leitmotif of eighteenth-century contractualism. Yet there, where nature played the role of a normative model, whether real or hypothetical, for the desired social constitution, this origin seems rather, in Marx, to mark a prehistory in which humanity has not yet achieved its destiny. In this context, we could go so far as to say that the reference to Aristotle's *Politics* is nothing more than a philosophical truism that convention has transformed into a cliché. But the use of the concept of *zoon politikon*, or the "political animal," the touchstone of Aristotelian naturalism, is a sign of Marx's cautious approach. For the founder of the Lyceum, to the extent that "nature . . . makes nothing in vain," and since humans are gifted with language, that is to say, with the ability to judge what is fair from what is not, the human being is then naturally a being who debates and acts as a member of a community, and not of a herd.[44] Naturalness is not a prior state of humanity, a historical presupposition, or a social norm of human action but is, rather, the condition of a humanity that only realizes its potential through the interactions of its members. The Marxian reference to Aristotle is, then, a means to

---

43   Marx, *Grundrisse*, 496.

44   Aristotle, *Aristotle's Politics*, trans. Benjamin Jowett (Oxford: Clarendon, 1908), 28.

break with contractualism and is an indicator of continuity in the naturalist tradition.

But there remains one problem: on the one hand, Marx seems to subscribe to the *naturalist* idea according to which the human being is, naturally, an animal capable of interacting with its kind; on the other hand, he does not consider this state to be a precondition of the individuation by which the human being is torn from a natural, tribal, herd-like, common origin but, rather, he considers it to be its *historical* result. How can nature be, at once, the origin from which human history has gradually been uprooted and the common condition of all humanity? How can history disconnect humanity from a given natural state while, at the same time, bringing about its intrinsic naturalness?

Historical Naturalism Versus Historicism

To answer, let us begin with the centrality accorded to "exchanges" between humans in the historical process of individualization.[45] To the extent that human history begins with the appearance of the individual, thought of as a member of a collectivity, then reciprocity becomes the relation by which each individual is at once the *unique* owner of that which is exchanged and a *member* of a community where goods circulate. Exchange is the process that transforms the herd members into a group of socialized individuals; and history is a process of individualization. At once, the actors of exchange are transformed into individuals, and the group into a society. Each person must be recognized now as an individual owner, and the relation between individuals produces a society where each person can conduct exchanges. However, the nature of what is exchanged remains uncertain. The Aristotelian reference that defined people as "political animals" could lead us to think that the exchange is of words as much as goods, of the symbolic as much as the material.[46] Yet, what can be said for certain is that the reciprocity of

---

45   Marx, *Grundrisse*, 496.
46   Marx thought first about the exchange of goods. See ibid.

exchange appears as one of the principal historical vectors of individualization and so the historicity of societies. Exchange is constitutive of the
social being (insomuch as society is the effect of a group of relations) and
of the history of societies (insomuch as history is the product of the
evolution of these exchanges). But our question can be asked in another
way. In what ways does this intrinsic historicity of exchange realize the
common condition of humanity? Or how does exchange assure "the
unity of living and active humanity with [their] natural, inorganic conditions"? Marx writes:

> Labour begins with a certain foundation—naturally arisen, spontane-
> ous, at first—then historic presupposition. Then, however, this foun-
> dation or presupposition is itself suspended, or posited as a vanishing
> presupposition which has become too confining for the unfolding of
> the progressing human pack.[47]

Note immediately that Marx substitutes the problem of production
for that of exchange. Human history begins by commerce that individu-
ates the members of the group and organizes society as a field of relations. But this intersubjective relation is always already a relation to the
land mediated by productive labor. Production, insomuch as it is a transformation of a given by which "man ... regulates and controls the
metabolism [*Stoffwechsel*] between himself and nature," is also a form of
exchange.[48] In the first case, exchange is commerce between humans
(*Verkehr*), and, in the second case, it is a material relation with nature
(*Wechsel*).[49] Production and commerce are two specific forms of
exchange, with nature and between humans, which are inseparable: relation to nature (production) is always mediated by property relations that

---

47   Ibid., 496–7.
48   Marx, *Capital*, 283.
49   "Der Wechsel" means change or difference. The expression "im Wechsel"
(each in turn) is exactly this idea of reciprocity and cycle inherent in the term
"Stoffwechsel" (metabolism). The translation of "Stoffwechsel" as "metabolism" is
necessary for the clarity it provides: for Marx, "der Stoffwechsel" is a synonym with
"das Metabolismus."

rule human relations (commerce), just as social relations always bear upon the way of appropriating and transforming natural materiality.

The "natural base" from which labor develops refers to the objective labor conditions (the land) but also the appropriation of natural wealth guaranteed by property relations based on how societies control their territory. However, this base, as Marx says above, "becomes a historical presupposition."[50] Empirically, this means that, little by little, human activity stopped developing strictly from the materiality that it found already there, and that it began to take the products of previous labor for its means and object of labor. From a philosophical point of view, the affirmation that the natural base becomes a historical given has a double meaning. For one, the transformed environment (nature is "produced" by human activity) becomes a "historical nature," to take up the expression of William Cronon and Jason Moore.[51] Nature is, at once, the ontological presumption and the historical result of social activity. But, at the same time, humanity itself has realized its potential and has developed its "essential powers."[52] In producing objects adapted for the satisfaction of its needs, humanity has met and increased its potential. Nature, which has been historicized by human activity, has a common history with humanity, which develops its potential in relation to the natural base. Marxian naturalism is, therefore, a "*historical* naturalism" where social formations belong to a nature that preexists them but in the midst of which they are transformed by interacting with it.[53]

Marx adds that the natural base—that is, the objective labor conditions and the property relations that determine the collective form of their

---

50   Marx, *Grundrisse*, 496.

51   William Cronon, "The Trouble with Wilderness; or, Getting Back to the Wrong Nature," in *Uncommon Ground: Rethinking the Human Place in Nature* (New York: W. W. Norton, 1995), 69–90; Jason W. Moore, *Capitalism in the Web of Life: Ecology and the Accumulation of Capital* (London: Verso, 2015).

52   Marx, *Economic and Philosophic Manuscripts of 1844*.

53   This concept is that of Frédéric Monferrand, and this argument in these pages develops from his book *La Nature du capital* (Paris: Amsterdam, 2024), 229. Many of which were put into print in the previously cited Paul Guillibert and Frédéric Monferrand, "Ecology/Ontology: A Contribution to Historical Naturalism," *Dialogue and Universalism* 3 (2018): 245–51.

appropriation—becomes an obstacle to the types of free development of human potential made possible through the growth of productive forces. The natural base would "become too confining for the unfolding of the progressing human pack," he writes. Even Marx's irony cannot make this coherent. The idea that universal history would free humanity from our natural origins is not consistent with the idea of the historicity of our separation from nature in class-based societies. The idea that communitarian societies would be more "natural" than those that come after them, and that these communitarian societies would come to limit the development of human potential, speaks to a form of historicism that considers past epochs as inferior stages of human development. This historicism considers the gradual distancing from communitarian forms to be a necessity, or "progress."

Two conflicting notions of history are seen in this text. On the one hand, nature is the precondition of all social history. The history of how humans relate to the land in classless societies is defined by the processual unity of their relation: unity is not only presupposed but held in place practically by the particular forms of production. The separation of nature from society is the contingent result of a history of private property. But in the *Grundrisse*, nature is also sometimes the *origin* that humanity must cast off in order to individuate; it is a "foundation [that is] too confining" for progress.

The first model is that of the historical socialization of nature; the second is that of a progressive denaturalization of history. The latter marks how Marx is debating with himself over a unilinear, teleological conception of history that progresses from an origin (that is natural and harmonious) toward an end (that is historical and conflict-free). Corresponding to these two notions of history are two antonymic definitions of nature: historicist evolutionism presents nature as the origin from which we must be emancipated; the theory of the multiplicity of historical times makes nature a permanent substratum of all socialization. The first is hardly compatible with the discovery of societies where communal property relations guarantee the sustainability of social metabolism. The second is, but it necessitates nevertheless the clarification of two essential aspects of historical materialism concerning the status of agrarian communes and their social ecology.

Marx's positions on communes would undergo two major shifts in the years following the writing of the *Grundrisse*. While the agrarian societies that he mentions in 1857–58 have already disappeared or been threatened with destruction, his exchanges with the Russian Narodniks and his readings in anthropology taught him about the deep history of contemporary rural Russian communes. The Greco-Roman and German communes had long been vanquished by real estate and private property; the Asian commune was resisting in places, but it could not hold out for long in the face of the destructive force of European colonialism. So, in 1870, the Russian commune, *mir*, or *obščina*, was still viable.[54] While worker revolutions in Europe had suffered important defeats (the movements of 1848, the Paris Commune), Marx was interested more and more in the Russian example. He learned Russian in mere weeks, and, thanks to his populist interlocutors, he discovered the existence of a revolutionary tradition that he would use to base the future of socialism on the development of agrarian communes.[55] His ethnographic research on Russian communes pushed him to pluralize his unilinear scheme of social time.[56]

The second inflection is due to his rereading of the agronomic works of Liebig and the botanic geography of Karl Fraas (1810–1875), which he undertook during the drafting of passages on rent for *Capital* in 1865 and 1866. These discoveries led him to abandon, once and for all, his

---

54 Vera Zasulich and Karl Marx, "1881 Letters of Vera Zasulich and Karl Marx," trans. and ed. Teodor Shanin, *Journal of Peasant Studies* 45, no. 7 (2018): 1183–202. Shanin notes that these English texts were translated from the French originals in *Marx-Engels Archiv* (1925) by Patrick Camiller who was "assisted at the stage of verification" by Perry Anderson, Derek Sayer, and Teodor Shanin.

55 Among his principal populist interlocutors were Nikolay Chernychevsky (1828–1889), Maksim Kovalevsky (1851–1916), and especially Pyotr Lavrov (1823–1900) and Nikolay Danielson (1844–1918), the translator of *Capital*. See, for example, the correspondence between Friedrich Engels and Karl Marx, *Lettres sur "Le Capital." Correspondance Marx-Engels*, trans. G. Badia, J. Chabbert, and P. Meier (Paris: Éditions sociales, 1964).

56 See, in particular, Teodor Shanin, "Late Marx: Gods and Craftsmen," in Teodor Shanin, ed., *Late Marx and the Russian Road: Marx and the Peripheries of Capitalism* (New York: Monthly Review, 1983), 3–39; and Kolja Lindner, ed., *Le Dernier Marx*, trans. Julien Guazzini (Toulouse: L'Asymétrie, 2019), 157–88.

progressivist definition of history. Putting a question about the capitalist perturbations of material exchange between nature and society at the center of his economic thinking about the production of value in agriculture, he made the ecological crisis into an inherent facet of the capitalist economy. Marx's earlier naturalist concepts were reworked and deepened by the discoveries of contemporary scientific ecology. Let us take up this trajectory with an analysis of the populist tradition with to which Marx became more committed in the 1870s.

Karl Marx in the *Obščina*

The Marxist conception of history has often been accused of being in league with a productivism whose role in the environmental crisis is now acknowledged. The string of environmental disasters of Soviet productivism would be the most evident sign of the aporias of Marx's naturalism. But to construct an ecological philosophy would suppose something else, namely, the reinvention of other socialist traditions founded in different cosmologies. For example, Joan Martínez Alier, one of the forerunners of economic ecology and the thinker behind the Vía Campesina, claims, while speaking of "ecological neo-Narodnism," to identify ecological, communalist, and indigenous movements that are part of a prior tradition, that of agrarian socialism.[57] Put simply, while Marxism is based on a modernist philosophy of technological development, Narodnism, or Russian populism, is a less dualistic cosmology centered on traditional communal organization. Narodnism would be, then, more fit for agrarian collectivism, more agile in the fight for the reappropriation of indigenous lands, and more favorable for the preservation of the environment. The invention of ecological socialism would urge us to rediscover Russian populism, not Marxist communism.

---

57 Beginning in the 1980s, Joan Martínez Alier defended the project of "ecological neo-Narodnism." See in particular Joan Martínez Alier, "The EROI of Agriculture and Its Use by the Via Campesina," *Journal of Peasant Studies* 38, no. 1 (January 2011): 145–60.

Yet, this caricatural opposition prolongs a Soviet historiography that built an antagonism between worker communism and agrarian socialism, which was strategic for its quest for power. The richness of the scientific and political ecologies of the first years of the Russian Revolution bears witness to the importance of communism's relations to the land in the 1920s.[58] To be sure, the historiographical opposition between Marx and the *narodniki* ignores the discussions, exchanges, and interactions that profoundly marked their respective trajectories on agrarian and communal questions. This Marx is not the one we most commonly see in his own work, and it is not the one that has inspired many communist thinkers after him. Most of the texts studied here remained in draft form, undiscovered until the beginning of the twentieth century, and in some cases were not published until the 1960s. We are interested not in confirming the *truth* of the "last Marx" or the "mature Marx"[59] but in proposing a "minor Marx" or "minoritarian Marx," for all intents and purposes unknown during his lifetime and ignored by those who followed him. Before I explain the nature of the exchanges between Marx and Russian populists, it is necessary to understand the nature of the *narodnichestvo* and its relevance for agrarian and environmental questions. According to Teodor Shanin, philosophers and political theorists fail to have the audacity required to conceive of the unity of revolutionary populism. To the extent that it can mean almost "anything from a revolutionary terrorist and a philanthropic squire," he writes, "the label of 'populist' . . . is badly lacking in precision."[60]

In short, the *narodnichestvo* characterizes a heterogeneous group of theoretical and political traditions, individual and collective trajectories, public and clandestine presses and publishers, which shaped

---

58   For example, see the foundational works of Vladimir Ivanovitch Vernadsky, particularly *The Biosphere*, ed. Mark A. S. McMenamin, trans. D. B. Langmuir (1929; repr., New York: Copernicus, 1998); or the theories of agrarian socialism of Alexander Vassilievitch Chayanov, *The Theory of Peasant Economy*, ed. Daniel Thorner, Basiel H. Kerblay, and Robert E. F. Smith, trans. unknown (1966; repr., Madison: University of Wisconsin Press, 1986).

59   Lindner, *Le Dernier Marx*; Louis Althusser, *Pour Marx* (Paris: Maspero, 1974), 26.

60   Shanin, *Late Marx*, 8.

forms of Russian socialism from the failure of the Decembrist Revolt of 1825, the symbolic date of its birth, to the assassination of Tsar Alexander II in 1881, which marks the height of the movement and the beginning of its decline. The debates over the abolition of serfdom (proclaimed May 3, 1861) crystallized the theoretical conflicts and the political antagonisms of nineteenth-century Russia. According to Franco Venturi, we can isolate specific configurations in the thought of Alexander Herzen (1812–1870) that appeared with regularity in almost all *narodniki*:

> The fundamental elements of Russian Populism—distrust of all democracy; belief in a possible autonomous development of Socialism in Russia; faith in the future possibilities of the *obshchina*; the need to create revolutionaries who could dedicate themselves to the people— these were the principles Herzen clung to after his experiences in 1848, the ideals he created for the next generation.[61]

The strength of Venturi's argument is that he formulates a general definition of populism that, while based on the writings of the first generation (Herzen; Bakunin, 1814–1876), is also deeply faithful to the thinkers who would follow (Chernychevsky, 1828–1889; Mikhaylovsky, 1842– 1904). Of Venturi's four criteria, the first is without doubt the most universally shared by all nineteenth-century socialists and, due to this, merits the least attention here. Briefly, the distrust of democracy comes from the fear that parliamentary regimes would assure the integration of the proletariat in a republican apparatus that would functionally reproduce class relations and not abolish them. Yet, three other criteria define the specific shape of populist thought.

First, the "belief in a possible autonomous development of Socialism in Russia" testifies to the desire of the *narodniki* to pluralize the unilinear schemes of the European philosophy of history. In brief, the idea of an

---

61   Franco Venturi, *Roots of Revolution: A History of the Populist and Socialist Movements in Nineteenth-Century Russia*, trans. Francis Haskell (New York: Knopf, 1960), 35.

autonomous socialism springs, on the one hand, from the communitarian self-organization of political struggles founded on the proto-communist forms of the *artel* (cooperative) and the *obščina* (rural community) and, on the other hand, from the existence of a multiplicity of world-historical trajectories. No society mechanically follows any other. More precisely, the *historical* autonomy of the Russian path to socialism was derived from the *political* autonomy of the rural commune where the relations of non-capitalist production were upheld on a small scale.

Then, the *mir*, or the *obščina*, presents an original, traditional form of communal organization. Each family possessed a house, a bit of land, and livestock. The collection of these arable village or community lands (*volost*) was periodically redistributed (the Black Partition) among the community members according to the needs of each. The prairies were reassigned annually and often collectively farmed. To the extent that the majority of the reproductive tasks of group life were handled by the women or managed collectively, wage labor was yet to develop: "a village shepherd, the local guards, the welfare of the orphans, and often a school, a church, a mill, etc."[62] An assembly of the heads of families (a structure that reproduced the permanence of patriarchal power) organized different tasks, elected its officers, and collected taxes and duties. The political autonomy of the rural commune produced a temporality unlike that of capitalist development, and it explained the specificity of its history.

Finally, populism has a moral dimension. The heritage of Proudhonism profoundly marked the trajectory of thinkers who, beginning with Herzen or Mikhaylovsky, considered the revolutionary experience as a practice of individual subjectivation that presupposes a certain type of character, which the hero of Chernychevsky's novel *What Is to Be Done?* would represent for a long time.[63] Populism's moral, and almost

---

62 Shanin, *Late Marx*, 11.

63 Nikolay Chernychevsky, *What Is to Be Done?*, trans. Michael R. Katz (Ithaca, NY: Cornell University Press, 1989.) Mikhaylovsky, leader of the second generation of populists, played a large role in the development of revolutionary populism in Russia as the person who presented Marx to Russians. He developed a subjectivist philosophy of history where individual mores predispose revolutionary action.

religious, support for the revolution is explained in part by its "subjective method."[64] The populist position is that revolutionary activity presupposes a specific subjectivity, namely, the capacity to break from the chains of the world to "go among the people," according to Bakunin's turn of phrase in "A Few Words to My Young Brothers in Russia."[65]

For Shanin, the terrorist faction of the People's Will (Narodnaya Volya), which emerged in 1879 by splitting from the group Land and Liberty (Zemlya I Volya), was "the most dramatic political expression" of the revolutionary experience in Marx's times.[66] The People's Will chose direct action and "terrorism," while the Black Partition (*Tcherny Peredel*) threw its weight behind propaganda and countryside agitation. Defined in these terms, revolutionary populism differs from the main two contemporary theories of development in Russia. It refuses Slavophile belief in "the innate specificity (not to say intrinsic supremacy) of Russia," and, at the same time, it opposes the idea of the "liberal's propagation of West European capitalism as Russia's bright future."[67] The possibility of autonomous development is part of a national and global analysis. Revolutionary populists believed that small-scale uses of the rural commune's collective property in the context of an already-globalized capitalism would open many different paths toward a better world. In sum, their analysis of the Russian state structure led them to affirm the uniqueness of a country where the central institutions still had the peasantry hobbled beneath its despotic yoke. They concluded that the state was not only the holder of power but also the "*main capitalist force*, both the defender and the creator of the contemporary exploitive classes."[68] The most concise summary of revolutionary populism is found in the belated party platform of the People's Will. The

---

64   The expression is Mikhaylovsky's. See James H. Billington, *Mikhailovsky and Russian Populism* (New York: Oxford University Press, 1958), 31.

65   Mikhail Bakunin, "A Few Words to My Young Brothers in Russia" (1869), in *The Basic Bakunin: Writings, 1869–1871*, ed. Robert M. Cutler (Buffalo, NY: Prometheus: 2010), 160–5, 164.

66   Shanin, *Late Marx*, 8.

67   Ibid., 8–9.

68   Ibid., 9.

preamble of the 1879 "Program of the Workers' Organization of People's Will" states the following:

1) the land and the implements of labor must belong to the whole people, with each worker using them as of right;
2) labor is produced not individually, but socially (through the communes (*obshchina's*) and cooperative (*artel's*) associations;
3) the products of communal labor must be shared, by their own decision, among all workers, according to the needs of each;
4) the State system must be based on a federative alliance of all the *obshchina's*;
5) every *obshchina* is fully independent and free in its internal affairs.[69]

This programmatic text reveals several essential aspects of the populist *obščina*. First, the *obščina* marks where in the countryside the collective reappropriation of land and the means of labor take place against the backdrop of the increasing development of private property. It is the best-suited organizational form for the political project of the socialist transformation of property relations and the production process. "Going to the people" presupposed a political philosophy of communal autonomy and Proudhon-inspired national federation. Russian populism was characterized by theoretical syncretism where autochthonous revolutionary traditions combined with French socialism and, later, with a Marxist critique of property relations. Russian populism is sometimes difficult to differentiate from certain anarchistic elements that are almost always found within it. (Case in point, Bakunin, and how he coined the catchphrase, "Go to the people!") We can see why contemporary ecological authors often take inspiration from populism in order to reinvent communalist traditions: the political and economic autonomy of the

---

69 "Program for the Workers Organization of the People's Will (excerpts)," in ibid., 231–2. [Translator's note: This list does not include the sixth statement in the preamble's program, that "every member of an *obschina* is entirely free in his convictions and personal life" (ibid., 232).]

commune is the basis of an agrarian collectivism and a state federalism, both based on the material and cultural reappropriation of territory. The peasantry is the principal revolutionary subject, and the countryside is the natural base of socialism. To evaluate the connections between Narodnism and Marxism presupposes common traits within this heterogenous movement (one approach's revolutionary strategy linked to the specificity of the Russian path toward socialism in the *mir*); and this asks us to set aside the historiography inherited from Stalin, which presented Marx as a thinker indifferent to the countryside peasantry and its concerns.

Engels was always more reluctant than Marx to support the populist argument regarding the autonomous development of communism in Russia. He began a tradition that accentuates the differences between Marx and the autochthonous tradition of Russian socialism. Venturi writes:

> In a conversation with N. F. Danielson in the 1890s, it was Engels's role to firmly state that, in reality, capitalism had already prevailed in Russia and that the country had already taken the route that the West had before it. The populist hypothesis will be pushed to the side. Instead, when he co-signed with Engels (who seems to have been the editor) the preface to the second Russian edition of the *Communist Manifesto* in 1882, a new idea seemed to be animating Marx: the one revolution that could save the *obščina* would come about only if the West became the necessary example and inspiration to a social transformation that would go beyond capitalism.[70]

This citation is striking in three ways. First, the dissolution of noncapitalist property relations appears as an already-achieved reality within the *obščina* rather than a current trend. This first interpretative difference can be accounted for in the temporal distance between Marx's

---

70 Franco Venturi, *Les Intellectuels, le Peuple et la Révolution. Histoire du populisme russe au XIXe siècle*, vol. 1, trans. Viviana Pâques (Paris: Gallimard, 1972), 46. [Translator's note: This passage does not exist in previous English translation.]

writings in the 1870s and 1880s and Engels's responses in the 1890s. Over the course of these decades, capitalism developed greatly, preventing any form of communist development in rural Russia. In fact, beginning in the 1870s, the "general" had refused the possibility of socialism's autonomous development in Russia.[71] In 1872, his dispute with Pyotr Tkachev and Bakunin set Engels off as a firm critic of the populist trajectory. In "Introduction to the Pamphlet *On Social Relations in Russia*" (1875), Engels presents ideas that he would never relinquish: the capitalist future of the rural commune is inevitable; only a socialist revolution in Russia based on a worker revolution in Western Europe would be able to save the collectivism of the *mir*.[72]

Second, for Engels, the future of Russia was inevitably Europe's past. The belief in the impossibility of achieving communism without first experiencing the detour of capitalism is itself in keeping with the linear and progressivist philosophy of history in which all social formations follow the steps borrowed from the most advanced European countries. It's truly remarkable that Engels used expressions so close to those of Marx in the 1850s, when Marx, speaking against the colonial violence of the British in India, recognized its imperial necessity.[73] For example, Engels wrote to Danielson:

> But history is about the most cruel of all goddesses, and she leads her triumphal car over heaps of corpses, not only in war . . . And we men and women are unfortunately so stupid that we never can pluck up

---

71   The "General" was the nickname given by Marx's daughters to Engels, due to his character and his tactical wishful thinking. See, in particular, Tristam Hunt, *Marx's General: The Revolutionary Life of Friedrich Engels* (New York: Picador, 2010).

72   Engels writes, "It is clear that communal ownership in Russia is long past its period of florescence and, to all appearances, is moving towards its disintegration." See Friedrich Engels, "On Social Relations in Russia," in Karl Marx and Friedrich Engels, *Collected Works*, ed. J. Cohen, M. Cornforth, and M. Dobb, vol. 24 (London: Lawrence & Wishart, 2010), 39–50 (48).

73   Karl Marx, "The Future Result of British Rule in India," in Karl Marx and Friedrich Engels, *Collected Works*, ed. J. Cohen, M. Cornforth, and M. Dobb, vol. 12 (London: Lawrence & Wishart, 2010), 217–22.

courage to a real progress unless urged to it by sufferings that seem almost out of proportion.[74]

These points, highly inflected with rhetorical flair, must be read in the context of his dispute with Danielson, one of the most important populists of the time, and someone who was strongly attached to Mikhaylovsky's "subjective method." This passage also reads as praise for capital's capacity to cause "sufferings that seem almost out of proportion."[75] Only a teleological philosophy of history where suffering is one moment in the progression toward salvation—that is, only a secularized theodicy—allows us to understand his paradoxical apologia for such violence.

Third, this unilinear philosophy is equally Eurocentric in that it believes that Europe points out the path forward and that no social formation can hope to follow its path without the help of Western industrialized countries. While playing on the polysemy of the word "direction," we could say that the meaning of history indicates which societies must *direct* the world. Chronological succession is the yardstick of strategic subordination to the political world. We find an undeniable proof of this Eurocentrism in the use—provisional in Marx, authoritative in Engels—of the concept of Oriental despotism:

Such complete isolation of diverse communes each from the others is reproduced in the same way from one end of the country to the other and brings about exactly the inverse of the common interest: it forms the natural base of *Oriental despotism*.[76]

We recognize in Engels's writing certain themes of Marx from the 1850s.[77] This political Orientalism presupposes and thus reproduces a

---

74   Friedrich Engels, "Engels to Nikolai Danielson in St. Petersburg [24 February 1893]," in Karl Marx and Friedrich Engels, *Collected Works*, ed. J. Cohen, M. Cornforth, and M. Dobb, vol. 50 (London: Lawrence & Wishart, 2010), 112.

75   Ibid.

76   Engels, "On Social Relations in Russia," 46.

77   Karl Marx, "The Future Result of British Rule in India," in Marx and Engels, *Collected Works*, vol. 12, 125–33.

unity of the East (the Orient) founded on its immemorial lack of change, and it permitted Engels to thrust Russia into an archaic Asia that only Europe would be able to wake from its torpor.[78] To the extent that the Russian Empire is only one variant of Oriental despotism, there is no specific path toward socialism that is possible for it.

The necessity of capitalism in Russia, a teleological philosophy of history, and Eurocentrism constitute the three epistemological obstacles that have, for a long time, complicated the interpretations of Marx's relation to populism. Beyond the well-known Leninist polemics, it was Stalinism that set in stone this opposition through exegetical dogmatism:

> The official theory was expressed by E. Jaroslavskij; while addressing the youth in 1937, he said, "The young members of the Party and Komsomol don't sufficiently know or always appreciate the meaning of the struggle that our party, overcoming the influence of populism, led against populism, branding it *as the principal enemy of Marxism* and the entire mission of the proletariat."[79]

In just a handful of years, populists went from being the principal Russian revolutionary tradition (for Marx) to the "principal enemy of Marxism" (for Stalinism). The formulation of this political opposition between Bolsheviks and Socialist Revolutionaries explains much about the purification of agrarian socialism within Marxism in Stalin's time. Yet, Marx's interactions with populists show how his work grew to incorporate their ideas. Narodnism contributed to the emergence of "multi-linear themes" in Marx's philosophy of history;[80] and multilinear history, which in no small part shaped Marx's ecological reflections, comes from his analysis of human relations to land.

---

78   Kevin B. Anderson, *Marx at the Margins: On Nationalism, Ethnicity, and Non-Western Societies* (Chicago: University of Chicago Press, 2010).

79   Venturi, *Les Intellectuels, le Peuple et la* Révolution, 19. Emphasis added. [Translator's note: This passage does not exist in previous English translation.]

80   Anderson, "From the *Grundrisse* to *Capital*: Multilinear Themes," in *Marx at the Margins*, 154–95.

The Ecology of the Russian Commune

Populist debates grew polarized around the future of agrarian collectivism. We could summarize the problem in the following manner: Was the *obščina* doomed to collapse through the body blows of capitalist development (the position of the Russian liberals and of Engels)? Or was it one element of a possible regeneration of Russia (the position of the Slavophiles)? Or, even, was it the strategic launching point for a socialist revolution (the position of populist revolutionaries)? Marx broached these questions in the 1870s, as much due to his personal interest in them as in order to respond to his Russian interlocuters. The failure of the Paris Commune led him to reorient his theoretical and strategic interests toward Russia, where he believed to exist the epoch's strongest revolutionary tendencies. Marx's response to the central problem of the intelligentsia consisted in showing the contradictory nature of this form of collective property: a contradiction between non-capitalist property relations (under-developed productive forces that were potentially superior to all others), and uneven global development, which plunged the agricultural commune into the world of capital's contradictions. Reading his texts on the *mir* also reveals that Marx considered this bipolarity (becoming communist or capitalist) to be based on a bad use of these modal categories in the philosophy of history: having choice is necessary, and yet each choice is contingent. In other words, if it's necessary for the commune to become either capitalist or communist, nothing indicates with any certitude what will in fact take place. This is the meaning of the incessant Marxist critiques that take exception to populism's "fatalist" readings of *Capital*.

Marx's most nuanced position on the agricultural commune can be found in his letter (and in its three drafts) to Vera Zasulich dated March 8, 1881. Zasulich (1849–1919) was a young combatant in Land and Liberty who had participated in the failed assassination of the military governor of St. Petersburg in 1878. Land and Liberty practiced and preached "terrorist" tactics to destabilize the autocratic regime. After this attempt failed, she took refuge in Switzerland and helped found Black Partition with Axelrod and Plekhanov in 1879. This group renounced revolutionary terrorism and adopted political agitation as a modus operandi. Afterward, Zasulich participated in the formation of the first Russian Marxist group, Emancipation of Labor, and was active alongside the Mensheviks in 1917. Before all of that, in 1881, she wrote to Marx about *Capital*. And while many essential elements of the three drafts were removed before he sent his letter, the letter's opening was practically the same as in his first draft. This consistency bears witness to the certainty that Marx felt that there could be no backtracking on the critique of historical fatalism.

The Drafts and the Letter to Vera Zasulich Dated March 8, 1881

In short, the question asked by Zasulich bore directly upon the "historical necessity" of capitalist development. Most Russian contemporaries had interpreted the history of primitive accumulation in determinist and linear terms:

> You know better than anyone how urgent this question is in Russia . . . and above all for our socialist party . . . Nowadays, we often hear it said that the rural commune is an archaic form condemned to perish by history . . . Those who preach such a view call themselves your disciples *par excellence*: "Marxists" . . . So you will understand, Citizen, how interested we are in Your opinion. You would be doing us a very great favor if you were to set forth Your ideas on the possible fate of our rural commune, and on the theory that it is historically necessary for every country in the world to pass through all the phases of capitalist production.[81]

All of the populists with whom Marx had been in correspondence since the 1870s were dubious about his philosophy of history. More than anything else, they needed to know whether Marxism was compatible

---

81   Zasulich and Marx, "1881 Letters," 1184.

with a theory of the multiplicity of historical trajectories, without which his thought would be useless in the context of tsarist Russia. The theory of unilinear historical progression derives generally from the historicism of the philosophy of history, but, more specifically, from a passage in the chapter in *Capital* on "so-called primitive accumulation."

In the German edition of 1867, Marx had insisted on the centrality of English history in the first process of accumulation. Despite the variety of forms that it would take across the world, primitive accumulation— the birth of capitalism—always corresponds to three phenomena: (1) the separation of laborers from their means of production by an act of dispossession; (2) the transformation of labor power into commodity and the inauguration of capitalist property relations; (3) the accumulation of capital. We see here how the expropriation of the land, insomuch as it furnishes the conditions of production and subsistence, provides the origins of capitalism. It's by this dispossession of the natural conditions of reproduction that capitalists come to enshrine market dependence.[82] Land appropriation sets off the commodification of natural commons and labor power.

At the end of volume 1, Marx's objective was to identify the provenance of the capitalist mode of production. His problem was the following: the advent of capitalist property relations corresponds to a massive accumulation of value; but, for accumulation to be possible, there must already exist capitalist social relations without which money could not be transformed into capital. Capital *as social relation* is the condition of the possibility of the accumulation of capital. Trying to escape this "vicious circle," which is equally logical and historic, Marx would concentrate on the case of England.[83] The history of *enclosures* gave him a historical example of the transition to capitalism:

> The expropriation of the agricultural producer, of the peasant, from the
> soil is the basis of the whole process. The history of this expropriation

---

82   Ellen Meiksins Wood, *The Origin of Capitalism* (New York: Monthly Review, 1999).
83   Marx, *Capital*, 850.

assumes different aspects in different countries, and runs through its various phases in different orders of succession, and at different historical periods. Only in England, which we therefore take as our example, has it the classic form.[84]

The existence of phases through which each society must pass is an idea derived from a linear scheme of history, which confirms the idea of an English *model* ("classic form"). The Eurocentrism of this passage, or rather its "methodological internalism," is undeniable.[85] Indeed, Marx tried to relativize this schema by stating that different phases of historical evolution can follow in different eras, in a different order, and with "different colorations." At the same time, he did not linger on the possibility that historical trajectories could be truly *singular*. Like many other Russian authors, Zasulich was worried about the validity of Marxist thought in the context of the *mir*: she was worried about what Marxism's triumph would mean for Russia.

However, this historical Eurocentrism correlates to "agrarianism" in the study of the relations of production. As the British historian David Omrod notes, volume 1 presents a solution that is "agrarian, productivist, and rooted in the class structure of rural society."[86] Marx's solution in 1867 is "productivist" not in the sense that it would serve as an apologist for technological development but because it privileges the study of

---

84 Ibid., 876.

85 In *How the West Came to Rule*, Alexander Anievas and Kerem Nişancıoğlu identify systematically the three bases of Eurocentrism. First, it derives from a "methodological internalism" that, while centered on Europe, regards the "rest of the world" as nothing but a point of comparison, and "in its worst form, this can lend itself to an interpretation of European society and culture as somehow superior to the rest of the world." A second presupposition follows: "The historical priority [of Europe] which articulates the historical distinction between tradition and modernity through a spatial separation of 'West' and 'East.' " Finally, a third "predictive proposition" emerges, that of "linear developmentalism" in which "endogenous processes of social change . . . are conceived as universal stages which encompass all societies of the world." See Anievas and Nişancıoğlu, *How the West Came to Rule: The Geopolitical Origins of Capitalism* (London: Pluto Press, 2015), 4–5.

86 David Omrod, "RH Tawney and the Origins of Capitalism," *History Workshop Journal* 18, no. 1 (September 1984): 138–59 (150).

the relations of *production* over the study of exchange and *circulation*, which will be a theme in volume 3. Although the history of colonization and the pillaging of the Americas occupies an important place in this chapter, Marx studies, in particular, the emergence of the relations of capitalist production in the English countryside between the fifteenth and eighteenth centuries. However, Marx's agrarianism in the chapter on "primitive accumulation" explains in part the infatuation of populists with *Capital* where they found a theory of historical development of the countryside as well as a Eurocentric philosophy in which the epistemic primacy accorded to England is accompanied by a historical determinism in reference to the rest of the world. Still, in his response to Zasulich, Marx cited not the German edition of 1867 but the French one of 1872:

> [Primitive accumulation] was accomplished in a *radical way* only in England: this country will thus necessarily play the leading role in our sketch. But all the other countries of *Western Europe* follow the same movement, although, according to the milieu, it changes with local color, or contracts, or presents a less strongly pronounced character, or follows a different order of succession.[87]

The publishers of the *Marx-Engels-Gesamtausgabe* consider this evolution the result of Marx's reading on the Russian situation and his interactions with populists. "Apparently influenced by his thinking on Russian agrarian relations from the beginning of the 1870s," the publishers write, "Marx modifies his conclusions in the French edition."[88] Between the editions of 1867 and 1872, two essential differences warrant reconsideration.

First, England is no longer the model or the vanguard for all of world history, but the social formation where the transition to capitalism was

---

87   Karl Marx, *Le Capital*, vol. 1, trans. J. Roy (1969; repr., Paris: Flammarion, 2014), secs. 5–8, 279. Emphasis added. [Translator's note: Translation is from the French, which was revised and rewritten by Marx himself; the English version of *Capital* does not include this passage.]

88   Friedrich Engels and Karl Marx, *Karl Marx, Friedrich Engels. Gesamtausgabe*, Abteilung II, vol. 10, *Das Kapital: Kritik der politischen Ökonomie* (1890) (Berlin: Dietz, 1991), 22.

the most radical. In other words, social relations were disrupted here more than elsewhere by capitalism and colonial conquest. The English case's centrality was a methodological commonplace: to understand the nature of capitalism presupposes studying the social formations that were changed the most profoundly by capitalism. Then, if there was a historical inevitability to capitalism, it's now linked only to European countries. The hesitancy of the German edition of 1867 is not seen in 1872. "Historical inevitability" is restricted to European countries and does not apply to the rest of the world. As he explained to Zasulich in 1881, the historical inevitability of Europe (the necessity of capitalism) is explained by the omnipresence of personal property there. The transition to capitalism on the continent is nothing other than the passage from one form of private property to another, the first based on individual labor and the second "based on the exploitation of another's work."[89] In rural, agrarian Russia, however, private property was still underdeveloped. Its future could not be the same as in other countries. Whether pushing the state toward capitalism or communism, the Tsarist Empire would take paths that none had taken before.

The irritation and malaise so evident in this letter mark the ambivalence of Marx's position in respect to the populist position. On the one hand, Marx drastically modified his unilinear philosophy to honor the theme of historical difference, which was dear to populists. But, on the other hand, he reproached them, sometimes virulently, for finding in his thought a Eurocentric philosophy of history that he had already abandoned, following their critiques. His famous letter of 1877 to Mikhaylovsky bears witness to his annoyance on this score.

Letter of 1877 to the Editors of *Native Notes*

Nikolay Mikhaylovsky (1842–1904) was one the most important populist leaders. Marx's letter to him was a response to Mikhaylovsky's defense of *Capital* against liberal detractors, in which Mikhaylovsky nevertheless

---

89   Zasulich and Marx, "1881 Letters," 1189.

accused Marx's unilinear philosophy of history of not leaving any place for Russia. The chief editor of the St. Petersburg literary journal *Native Notes* (*Otétchestvenniye Zapiski*) accused Marx of overreach: "Your place is not in Russia, but in Europe, and here you are only interfering and fighting with windmills."[90] The sudden reference to Cervantes's *Don Quixote*, which held a special place for Marx, made Mikhaylovsky's irony clear. The "knight with the sad face" fights against windmills that he mistakes for giants. This illusion can be interpreted as an illustration of the historical disconnect between the chivalric ideology of the feudal past and the preindustrial development of productive forces. However, it's precisely this lack of connection that Mikhaylovsky ironically mobilized in his critique of Marx's philosophy of history. Marx studied the historical trajectory of Western Europe, and so his analysis would not fit the Russian situation, where the productive forces of industrial capital were just as absent as giants in Cervantes's novel.

In his response, Marx agreed with Mikhaylovsky on the impossibility of universal history. But he took issue with the notion that the populist found in "his historical sketch of the genesis of capitalism in Western Europe . . . a general historical-philosophical theory whose highest virtue would be its supra-historicity."[91] The Marxist history of capitalism is a European history that does not have anything to say about the historical trajectory of non-capitalist social formations. "The chapter on primitive accumulation does not pretend to do more than trace the path by which, in Western Europe, the capitalist order of economy emerged from the womb of the feudal order of economy," Marx writes.[92] In 1877, Marx was already defending points that he would make in his letter to Zasulich in 1881. But in his letter, his position on the Russian agricultural commune was only sketched out. Mikhaylovsky's error consisted in scanning *Capital* for a philosophy of history, and he went just as far in pursuing a one-sided reading that could not deal with the contradictions that structure the

---

90   Billington, *Mikhailovsky and Russian Populism*, 66.

91   Marx, Engels, and Lenin, *Sur les sociétés précapitalistes*, 351–2.

92   Karl Marx, "Letter to *Otechestvenniye Zapiski*," in Marx and Engels, *Collected Works*, vol. 24, 196–201.

obščina, the global market, and the capitalist development of technology. Yet, it would only be in his drafts and the eventual letter to Zasulich that Marx would find the means to lay out in full the social significance and contradictory nature of the Russian rural commune.

The Unequal Development of Communal Ecology

In keeping with his analyses of precapitalist formations in the *Grundrisse*, Marx discovered in the *mir* a form of the communal land ownership that was not specifically Russian but much more widespread. What changed in the Russian case was the fact of this archaic form's persistence within contemporary capitalism, as well as the strategic role that it might play in the case of revolutionary uprisings. The three drafts of Zasulich's letter in 1881 show the complexity of his opinions on the *mir*.

Different from populists, Marx considered dispersion, localism, and the autonomy of the rural commune as signs of its weakness vis-à-vis centralized power rather than as strengths in the context of social struggle. Moreover, the *mir* was influenced by industrial capitalism, which transformed "the inherent dualism" of the agricultural commune to produce a historical contradiction:[93]

> [Communal property] and all the resulting social relations provide it with a solid foundation, while the privately owned houses, fragmented tillage of the arable land and private appropriation of its fruits all permit a development of individuality incompatible with conditions in the more primitive communities. It is just as evident, however, that the very same dualism may eventually become a source of disintegration.[94]

In Marx's time, more than three-fifths of the arable land in western Russia was owned by villages.[95] But labor was rarely collective. Large

---

93   Zasulich and Marx, "1881 Letters," 1191.
94   Ibid.
95   Shanin, *Late Marx*, 11.

parcels of land being worked collectively were being replaced by plots cultivated by individual farmers. In his first draft of his letter to Zasulich, the double character of the *obščina*—collective property and communal division of the land on the one hand, and piecemeal labor on the other— presented the dual advantage of guaranteeing the existence of non-capitalist social relations while partially satisfying modern aspirations for the rights of the subject. The development of individuality neverthe-less led to a patriarchal reaction in the commune that put the brakes on modern tendencies due to the fear of the male heads of households losing power. As Shanin notes, "Marx had no doubts about the limita-tions of the 'archaic' commune: material 'poverty,' its parochiality and its weakness against external exploitive forces."[96]

In his view, the individualist dimension of the *obščina*, the parceling out of labor, and "the gradual growth of movable property [which begins with] their wealth in livestock" risked imperiling communal forms of property once again.[97] Marx presented the agricultural commune as a transitional form between the collective property of "archaic" societies and the modern world's conception of property as private real estate. According to Marx, the rural commune, a social formation in evolution, was fraught with contradictory tendencies. It maintained elements of agrarian collectivism from traditional societies, but it had also already assimilated the individual dimension of modern property relations. Yet again, Marx set himself up implicitly against the two dominant interpre-tations of the Slavophile controversy: the commune was neither an authoritarian invention of tsarist Russia to limit the development of capitalism, as Western liberals were given to say, nor was it a relic of old Russia, as the Slavophiles argued. It was a contradictory form where long-standing elements of collective property were modified by the inte-gration of individualist tendencies, leading to a new order that guaran-teed its "vigorous life."[98] But can we spot in it the form that property relations in the commune will take in the future?

---

96   Ibid., 15.
97   Zasulich and Marx, "1881 Letters," 1191n2.
98   Ibid., 1199.

Marx would have answered in the negative. For him, the end of the process underway in the Russian commune remained indeterminate and contingent. It might lead to privatization *or* to collectivization, depending on whether fragmented forms of labor organization or forms of communal property prevailed, respectively. He asked rhetorically in the first draft:

> But does this mean that the development of the "agricultural commune" must follow this route in every circumstance? Not at all. Its constitutive form allows of the following alternative: either the element of private property which it implies gains the upper hand over the collective element, or the reverse takes place.[99]

This passage invokes the problem of contingent futures, discussed so eloquently by Aristotle in chapter 9 of *On Interpretation*.[100] Aristotle uses the example of a battle at sea:

> A sea-fight must either take place to-morrow or not, but it is not necessary that it should take place to-morrow, neither is it necessary that it should not take place, yet it is necessary that it either should or should not take place to-morrow.[101]

Contradictory statements about the future have the "same character," Aristotle writes, "since they do not yet correspond with facts."[102] Yet, Marx maintained the validity of an unspoken third option, and he refused the fatalism inherent in the idea that the confrontation of historical tendencies would lead necessarily to the realization of one or the other. In his analysis of property relations in the *obščina*, Marx's premise

---

99   Ibid., 1192.

100   For a translation and commentary on chapter 9, see Jules Vuillemin, "Le chapitre IX du *De Interpretation* d'Aristote. Vers une rehabilitation de l'opinion comme connaissance probable des choses contingentes," *Philosophiques* 10, no. 1 (1983): 15–52.

101   Aristotle, "On Interpretation," trans. E. M. Edghill, in *The Works of Aristotle Translated into English* (Oxford: Oxford University Press, 1955), 71.

102   Ibid.

is the following: the commune would become either capitalist (if its tendencies toward the subdivision of large parcels of land into individual farming plots continued), or communist (if its collectivist tendencies won the day). Inasmuch as this polarity is an imposed structure, each of these two ways is possible. But Marx took pains to separate communitarian *property relations* from the *organizational forms* of piecemeal labor and the capitalist *historical milieu*. Thus, it was not "under the same relation" that the *mir* was communitarian and capitalist.[103] In the future, the question would resolve as follows: What were the factors that would push the *obščina* toward the one, or the other? Marx's answer begins from an analysis of the global context, the consideration of productive forces, and the revolutionary events that would allow (or not) the ongoing existence of collective property.

According to Marx, the rural commune was what is left over from large-scale agrarian collectivism, and it provided the inspiration to dream of a socialist transition in Russia. But the commune was also an ambivalent form that could be destroyed by its own capitalist tendencies. In the end, it was the "historical milieu" that was determinative.[104] Paradoxically, Russia's capitalist environment guaranteed the technological possibility of a communist future to the *obščina*. In his third draft of the letter to Zasulich, Marx commented on the signs of a possible future communist development of the *mir*:

> Communal land ownership offers it the natural basis for collective appropriation, and its historical context—the contemporaneity of capitalist production—provides it with the ready-made material conditions for large-scale cooperative labor organized on a large scale. It may therefore incorporate the positive achievements developed by the capitalist system, without having to pass under its harsh tribute.[105]

---

103   Aristotle, *The Metaphysics*, trans. Hugh Tredennick, book 4, part 3 (London: William Heinemann, 1933), 161.

104   In particular, see the second draft of his letter to Zasulich in Zasulich and Marx, "1881 Letters."

105   Zasulich and Marx, "1881 Letters," 1199.

Marx is remarking on the contemporaneity of the contradictory relations of production and productive forces. The archaic forms of communal property, a multifaceted tradition in transition, coexisted with the most recent mode of production—capitalism. Marx did not interpret this contemporaneity in evolutionary or historicist terms. The oldest social formations aren't merely chaff destined to be replaced by modern elements. Instead, the transitory nature of the agricultural commune, which had already brought the modern recognition of individuality into its piecemeal labor organization, was a contemporary of capitalism. The existence of different historical temporalities must, then, be understood to mean two things. First, it marks the coexistence of *singular histories* (the history of the primitive accumulation of capital in Europe and the separate history of the agricultural commune in Russia); second, it outlines the multiplicity of *possible futures* (capitalism or collectivism). The multiplicity of histories holds the future at bay. Meanwhile, this heterogeneity cannot be thought of in terms of the radical difference of absolute exteriority. The history of the Russian commune no longer exists side by side with the history of capital, but within it. The development of the global market makes capitalism the "historical milieu" in which individual histories take place. The interaction of heterogenous histories within the same global history produces contingent futures.

So, two questions had to be answered: What are the necessary resources for the maintenance of collectivism in the Russian commune? And, how can the capitalist historical milieu offer the necessary social resources for the preservation of collective property relations?

Marx ceded the populist point that Russia's development had been uneven and multifaceted. It was, rather, the combination of the old relations of production and the new productive forces that would allow the *mir* to be saved. While the concept of uneven development is already present in *Capital*, and while it would become one of the principal themes of Lenin's *The Development of Capitalism in Russia* and Trotsky's *History of the Russian Revolution*, it was first brought up by populists speaking about Russian culture. As James Billington has remarked, the theme dates to 1835 when the poet Pyotr Chaadaev wrote to Ivan Turgenev: "We advance more quickly than others because we came after them."[106]

Marx borrowed from the important Russian populist Chernychevsky the idea that "under the influence of the high development which a certain phenomenon of social life has attained . . . this phenomenon [can] rise from a lower level straight to a higher one, passing over the intermediate logical moments."[107] In practice, it was the immediate adoption of the most developed productive forces and the combination of these with precapitalist relations of production that would make it possible for the Russian rural commune to survive its individualist and redistributive tendencies. The uneven and heterogeneous development of communitarian relations of production (the "natural base") and the capitalist productive forces (the resources of the "historical milieu") allowed the possibility of a communist future for the *obščina*. Now the second question returns: What are the capitalist resources that would allow the Russian commune to maintain its property relations? In other words, how would the adoption of the most developed capitalist productive forces allow for the conservation of non-capitalist relations of production and the maintenance of its socio-ecological metabolism?

In his support for the Russian commune's adoption of the most developed productive forces, Marx seems to legitimize the critiques that many ecological thinkers have directed his way.[108] But criticism about his productivism rests on the equivalence of productive forces and technological development. Here, too, Marx's response is more complex than first meets the eye.

In the second draft of his letter to Zasulich, he wrote about the "machines" that would allow the agricultural commune to augment its productivity: "The physical configuration of the Russian land is eminently suited to machine-assisted agriculture, organized on a large

---

106   Billington, *Mikhailovsky and Russian Populism*, 70.

107   Nikolay Chernyshevski, "A Critique of Philosophical Prejudices against Communal Ownership," in Shanin, *Late Marx*, 188.

108   These include Serge Audier's nuanced and well-informed critique, *L'Âge productiviste. Hégémonie prométhéenne, brèches et alternatives écologiques* (Paris: La Découverte, 2019), 147–213.

scale and [in the hands] performed by co-operative labor."[109] While dealing with populists, Marx always acknowledged the specific agricultural environment of the Russian commune. In short, the *open field* and the scope of the surface area of village lands seemed to facilitate the development of an intensive mechanical agriculture capable of assuring a significant boost in productivity, and thus higher yields. Admitting a place for machines and fossil fuels bears witness to a modernist philosophy by which the technological domination of nature assures social development. However, Marx supported the integration of machines only to the extent that they were in the community's hands and reinforced cooperative labor. In his second draft, Marx wrote of the positive role that scientific and agronomic discoveries play in the development of communal labor:

> But where is the peasant to find the tools, the fertilizer, the agronomic methods, etc.—all the things required for collective labor? This is precisely where the Russian "rural commune" is greatly superior to archaic communes of the same type. For, alone in Europe, it has maintained itself on a vast, nationwide basis. It is thus placed within a historical milieu in which the contemporaneity of capitalist production provides it with all the conditions for co-operative labor. It is in a position to incorporate the positive achievements of the capitalist system, without having to pass under its harsh rule.[110]

While mechanical development per se is certainly in line with the productivist designs of intensive capitalist agriculture, "fertilizer" and "agronomic methods" were references to Justus von Liebig and his critique of unsustainable agriculture. We know that Marx was a dedicated reader of the German chemist, who considered capitalist agriculture to be a form of "pillage economy" (*Raubwirtschaft*), where the nutrients stripped from the soil would never return, thus leading to the soil's

---

109   Zasulich and Marx, "1881 Letters," 1194.
110   Ibid., 1194. Translation slightly altered.

progressive impoverishment.[111] Reading Marx's letter to Zasulich for its ecological content might seem rash if Marx had not brought up ecology several days earlier in a letter to Danielson. In his letter dated February 19, 1881, in which he readied himself to write to Zasulich, Marx wrote to the translator of *Capital* in the following terms:

> The soil being exhausted and getting not the elements—by artificial and vegetable and animal manure, etc.— to supply its wants, will, with the changing favour of the seasons, of circumstances independent of human influence—still continue to yield harvests of very different amounts, though, summing up a period of years, as for instance, from 1870–80, the stagnant character of the production presents itself in the most striking character.[112]

If it were still possible to doubt Marx's ecological thinking, the reference to the "artificial" fertilizers created by the German chemist confirms how Marx's interactions with populists in the 1880s were marked by an ecological approach to the issue of social metabolism. We have already seen his attention to this topic in 1857–58. However, with Marx's rediscovery of Liebig's agronomy in 1865–66, the idea of social metabolism was now more technological, and its usage, which was sometimes metaphorical in the 1850s, was now strictly about the material exchanges (*Stoffwechsel*) between organisms and their environment.[113] This material exchange implies a form of reciprocity between an organism or society and the environment, and thus the existence of a natural totality constituted by these exchanges. Marx thought of the natural environment as a world that

---

111   Justus von Liebig, *Die Chimie in ihrer Anwendung auf Agricultur und Physiologie* (1840), 9th ed. (1876; repr., Hom: Agrimedia, 1995).

112   Karl Marx, "Marx to Nikolai Danielson," in Karl Marx and Friedrich Engels, *Collected Works*, ed. J. Cohen, M. Cornforth, and M. Dobb, vol. 46 (London: Lawrence & Wishart, 2010), 60–5.

113   The use of Liebig in this way, to show the harmonious circulation of matter in flux between different "kingdoms" of life, is perfectly illuminated in Engels's letter to Lavrov on November 12, 1875. See Friedrich Engels, "Engels to Pyotr Lavrov. 12 November," in Karl Marx and Friedrich Engels, *Collected Works*, ed. J. Cohen, M. Cornforth, and M. Dobb, vol. 45 (London: Lawrence & Wishart, 2010), 106–10.

tended to balance itself out, and in which capitalist disruption appeared as an aberration. The metabolic disturbance of capitalism was a sign of pathological social relations.

In *Chemistry and Its Application to Physiology, Agriculture, and Commerce* (1840), Liebig discovered the role that nutrients in the earth like nitrogen, phosphorous, and potassium play in plant development.[114] He set up the first systematic study of soil's organic and inorganic components to understand the balance necessary for healthy plant development. Liebig understood that adding organic substances or nitrogen could not guarantee maximum crop yields at harvest if other essential elements were missing in the soil. He discovered the first law of agronomy, which he called the "law of the minimum": plant development is limited by the scarcest nutrient, and so farmers must bear this in mind while planting. He wrote of the primary importance of minerals and inorganic substances. In short, plants can directly absorb organic material present in the atmosphere and rainwater. But they can only absorb inorganic substances through their roots, that is, through the soil. These inorganic substances (composed of metals, yet containing no carbon—the basic element of life) are present in limited quantities in the soil. Liebig's chief concern was to limit the leaching or loss of inorganic substances from the soil. To increase harvests in a sustainable way, whatever minerals are absorbed from the soil by the plants in the course of their growth has to be returned to the soil. This is the second law that Liebig formulated, the "law of replacement." In the seventh edition of this book (1862), he wrote of it in the following manner: "From this discovery comes in turn that we must return to the soil everything we've taken from it in order to preserve its fertility."[115] This law was, for Liebig, the basis or fundamental principle of "rational agriculture." In sum, Liebig insisted on the importance of respecting the balance of organic and inorganic substances in the soil as the basic principle for sustainable production.

---

114 Justus von Liebig, *Organic Chemistry and Its Application to Agriculture and Physiology*, ed. Lyon Playfair (London: Taylor & Walton, 1840).

115 Justus von Liebig, *Les lois naturelles de l'argiculture*, vol. 1 (Paris: A. Scheler, 1862), 24.

However, while previous editions of Liebig's work were still confident in the capacity of capitalist agriculture to reform itself in keeping with sustainability, the 1862 edition took a radical departure from that tone. This new edition was prefaced by an introduction in which Liebig showed himself to be extremely pessimistic: he believed that capitalist agriculture could lead only to a loss of fertility because it demanded profitability that did not respect the natural laws of the local environment.[116] It's this later edition that Marx reread while editing *Capital* in 1865–66 that would play a part in all of his future thinking on capitalist agriculture. Intensive agriculture did not permit the retention of the necessary amounts of nitrogen and phosphorous in the soil for continued fertility. Quite the opposite, in fact:

> [It] disturbs the metabolic interaction between man and the earth, i.e. it prevents the return to the soil of its constituent elements consumed by man in the form of food and clothing; hence it hinders the operation of the eternal natural condition for the lasting fertility of the soil . . . All progress in capitalist agriculture is a progress in the art, not only of robbing the worker, but of robbing the soil; all progress in increasing the fertility of the soil for a given time is a progress towards ruining the more longlasting sources of that fertility.[117]

We owe a debt to John Bellamy Foster and Paul Burkett for bringing up the central role that metabolic interaction plays in the environmental structure of capital.[118] Marx's ecological critique of capitalism is seemingly in contradiction with the second draft of his letter to Zasulich. By the "positive gains" of capitalism, Marx did not have in mind the infinite growth of production in capitalism's industrial development but rather

---

116   Justus von Liebig, "1862 Preface to Agricultural Chemistry," *Monthly Review* 70, no. 3 (July–August 2018).

117   Marx, *Capital*, 638.

118   See Paul Burkett, *Marxism and Ecological Economics: Toward a Red and Green Political Economy* (Chicago: Haymarket, 2009), and *Marx and Nature: A Red and Green Perspective* (New York: St Martin's Press, 1999); and John Bellamy Foster, *Marx's Ecology: Materialism and Nature* (New York: Monthly Review, 1999).

the scientific and agronomic results that could lead to increased agricultural productivity and the reestablishment of communal labor through the maintenance of collective property relations. Whatever productive forces Marx wished to see adopted by the commune nevertheless stopped short of the mechanization of agriculture; instead, he wished to see the peasants apply chemical, edaphological, and horticultural laws to farming. In the last paragraph of the third draft of the letter to Zasulich, we find a clear illustration of this thinking. Marx considered the "curious dismemberment" of cultivable lands into a multitude of little parcels to be "out of keeping . . . with agronomic laws."[119] While he acknowledged the rationality of this practice, which aimed to limit the vacillations in profitability due to differences of fertility between soils, and while he also admitted the possibility of a transition from a parcel-based model to collective exploitation, in either case plant chemistry was a new, rational tool for parcel-based peasant practices. In the environmental context of the Russian *open field*, scientific agronomy allowed the retention of communal ownership through generalizing agriculture techniques that were more favorable for collective labor. The development of capitalist productive forces pointed to social cooperation in peasant labor informed by scientific agronomic laws. The capitalist division of labor had to be replaced by producer cooperation.

The capitalist productive forces that Marx thought able to save collective relations on the *obščina* weren't those of the worst type of productivism, with its barns full of agricultural machines and fossil fuels. He pointed instead to scientific knowledge that assured the coherence between communitarian property relations and the collective labor process. It's undeniable that Marx's position here—his confidence in the agronomic science of his time and its corollary, his distrust for traditional peasant practices—might seem excessively modernist for a contemporary reader used to praise heaped on non-modern ways of life and critiques of Western science. But it's nevertheless important to note that Marx's perspective was not aimed at setting up an abstract opposition between rational modern science and traditional practices; rather, it

---

119 Zasulich and Marx, "1881 Letters," 1200. Translation slightly altered.

meant to show that the inherent rationality of parcel-based peasant labor practices in the Russian commune put in jeopardy the continuity of communal relations of production in global capitalism. Far from playing Western scientific rationality against an Oriental peasant archaism, he was intent rather on saving Russian communalism by the application of technical knowledge that would support the fight against the contradictions that capitalism introduced into the commune.

In the end, the continuity of the rural community would be possible only if a proletarian revolution intervened to limit the transformation of property relations. Marx and Engels were equally certain that agrarian socialism would be impossible without a worker communism capable of waging a struggle to prevent the large-scale transition to capitalism. By themselves, the communes did not have enough political power and technological knowledge to survive an autocracy, outside of capitalism's logic of profitability. Instead, "to save the Russian commune, there must be a Russian Revolution."[120] It was here that Marx's difference of opinion with Engels is the most important, since the latter thought that the revolution necessarily had to come from Western Europe. Marx considered the commune as one possible territorial base for Russian communism, should an urban worker revolution offer to the communes the opportunity to develop collectively in a more propitious historical milieu. His ethnographic and ecological studies convinced him that "for social regeneration in Russia . . . in order that it might function as such, the harmful influences assailing it on all sides must first be eliminated, and it must then be assured the conditions for spontaneous development."[121] Without a revolution, the communes would not be able to resist the economic logic of profit and the territorial power of the state.

The Russian path toward communism was based on the regeneration of the most "archaic" relics of the past. It was no longer a question of a unique path and some essential steps, but a contingent history where the contradictions of territoriality and globalization led to singular futures.

---

120   Ibid., 1196.
121   Ibid., 1191.

The archaic forms of peasant collectivism appeared as possible bases for communist development:

> The best proof that such a development of the "rural commune" corresponds to the historical trend of our epoch, is the fatal crisis . . . that will come to an end . . . with the return of modern society to a higher form of the most archaic type—collective production and appropriation.[122]

The socialist horizon wouldn't arise through a mechanical evolution of the present but as the revolutionary reinvention of the past.

Marx's history of property is far from being indifferent to ecology. Yet, some of the ways that he is used today tend to discount the importance of the *political moment*. In sum, the discovery of the metabolic nature of economic systems leads some to replay an ancient Marxist "economism" in a renovated form of "ecologism." Political and ideological institutions risk appearing as simple socio-economic metabolic reflections. Substituting ecology for economy, Marxists lay bare the "reductionism" that often characterizes their approach. Some write as though political practices were only effects determined *in the last instance* by material relations to nature. Indeed, these relations are no longer strictly economic, but certain Marxist commentators still give too little space to discursive traditions, representations, and imaginaries in the transformation of the new environmental regime. Materialist intervention in political economy must, then, avoid the trap of a too-rapid metamorphosis. An ecological revolution presupposes an ideological struggle, and historical naturalism must be able to produce strategies for a large number of symbolic socializations of the environment. This is why it is necessary to set forth a materialist theory of the cultures of nature.

---

122   Ibid., 1195.

3

Nature Doesn't Tell Stories: The Cultural Naturalism of Raymond Williams

Guy thought that the story told in this way made it sound as if the river had decided where to go . . . If you considered it carefully, even with all the power of its waters, the St. Lawrence had had to make do with the only bed possible. Its volition was only an idea, a restricted point of view that didn't take too many details into account. Similarly, he thought, men convince themselves that they have choices, but the road they take is always the only one at their disposal.

Guy was the river. He thought he had made the best decision, but only because it was the only one possible.

The river had had to open up the way to the sea so that it wouldn't dry up and die.

—Wu Ming, *Manituana*, trans. Shaun Whiteside

Imagining new relations with nature presupposes the invention of the collective property of all forms of life. Without this, the increasing dispossession of the means of subsistence will lead to ecological catastrophe and an exploitation of human labor that only ever increases. Classes are born through the expropriation of the natural conditions of life.

There can be no mistaking the following point: to transform the way life is organized and to acknowledge the seriousness of the ecological disaster we face, we have to accept that political practices must bear in mind non-humans and our relations with them. The essential conditions for the viability of the biosphere for human life are clear: We must preserve biodiversity or limit its all-too-rapid collapse; prevent the extinction of all forms of life; guarantee the stability of ecosystems; and prevent climate catastrophes. Revolutionary theory must, then, contemplate the place of these natural beings in the movement for the abolition of capitalism. Communism in the future will have to deal with the environmental conditions of human history, and it will have to try to bring about social conditions that lessen our disruption of the earth system.

Facing the climate catastrophe, we now realize that natures intervene in our histories. These interventions are not metaphorical: viruses, hurricanes, and fires disturb the ordinary functioning of societies. In different contexts, these natures produce unique events and condition social responses to varying degrees of efficacy. From the calamities of climate change to mushrooms growing at the end of the world, our era seems to be marked by the sudden emergence of realities that modern politics sought at every juncture to deny and suppress, and that now function as "quasi-intentional harbingers."[1] The silence of spring now pervades all the seasons. As the environmental historian William Cronon has written, "Nature and the universe do not tell stories."[2]

Although they affect the social world, that is, they sometimes seem "to have something to say," these entities have no means of speaking. Inasmuch as these phenomena do not speak (the mad cow does not, climate change does not, the matsutake mushroom does not) but have social effects, how can we make sense of their intervention in human histories? To write the ecological history of societies asks us to think about *the effects of social activities on the environment* but also *the effects of certain natural realities on social history*. But how can we conceptualize the reciprocal effects of social and natural histories, knowing that only

---

1 Stéphane Haber, *Critique de l'antinaturalisme. Études sur Foucault, Butler, Habermas* (Paris: PUF, 2006), 23.

2 William Cronon, "A Place for Stories: Nature, History, and Narrative," *Journal of American History* 78, no. 4 (March 1992): 1347–76 (1368).

humans talk? How can we speak of the role of climatic, biological, and geological events if they cannot speak for themselves? How can we integrate these silent non-humans into political practices?

To the extent that the appearance of these "natural" phenomena is always conditioned by cultural formations, these questions pose immediate complications. We confront an epistemological dead end: at once, we must evaluate the social effects of "nature" while, at the same time, given cultural history's ever-present conditioning of our perception of nonhuman realities, it seems difficult to recount the history of nature without mentioning the long history of its symbolic construction. We have to tell the story of "nature's effects" on the social world while presenting the historical structuration of our perception of naturalness; we have to evaluate the power of natures to act while acknowledging that these natures are already informed by cultural representations.

The idea that we can write a social drama in which the environment is a silent protagonist is not new. We see these dramas in literatures from all eras, from ancient times to nineteenth-century naturalism. In "Realism, Naturalism and their Alternatives," Raymond Williams writes the following:

> Thus naturalism, specifically associated with the new scientific natural history proposed as a matter of principle that it is necessary to describe (present, embody, realize) an environment if we wish to understand a character, since character and environment are indissolubly linked. Thus naturalist dramatists did not include detailed physical and social settings because it was technologically possible with new theatrical technology and resources, or because it was one kind of formal method as against others, but because they insisted that it was impossible to understand character and action unless the full physical and social environment which shaped character and action was directly presented, indeed as a kind of character and action in itself.[3]

---

3 Raymond Williams, "Realism, Naturalism, and Their Alternatives," *Ciné-Tracts* 1, no. 3 (Fall 1977–Winter 1978): 1–6 (2).

Today, nature's stark reminders make it impossible not to consider the "physical environment as signifying," and they invite us to investigate again the forms of writing of literary naturalism.[4] The presence in the naturalist drama of a new protagonist who silently acts opens the methodological possibility of a social history in which natures intervene in a spontaneous way, manifesting as cultural conditions.

Speak the Country: Cultural Learning and Material Economy

Beginning in the 1970s, Raymond Williams studied the role of literature in the construction of our social relation with nature. *The Country and the City*, his major work on this theme, sets out to trace the genealogy of changes between the city and the country in poetry, theater, and the English novel, from the eighteenth century to the twentieth century. His work lays out a way of thinking about discursive formations that define our sense of the real and condition our perception of nature. Following Williams's statement that "the idea of nature contains an extraordinary amount of human history," I want to show how certain aesthetic forms and "structures of feelings" are the product of the social experience of nature that they actively modify.[5] For the "founder" of cultural studies, nature is knowable through its cultural manifestations because socialized by language.[6] His project means to provide an immanent critique of culture from the history of the forms through which nature appears. His thinking about naturalism comes face to face with the problem of the conjunction between natural reality and its cultural perceptions.

In "Marxism and Culture," the concluding chapter of his seminal *Culture and Society*, Williams tried to elucidate the confusion that dominates Marxist thought on culture:

---

4   Ibid., 5.

5   Raymond Williams, "Ideas of Nature," in *Problems in Materialism and Culture: Selected Essays* (London: Verso, 1980), 70.

6   This status is debatable, due to the competing presence of the Birmingham School. See, in particular, Paul Jones, *Raymond Williams's Sociology of Culture: A Critical Reconstruction* (London: Palgrave Macmillan, 2004), xiv.

Yet, in one way or another, the situation will have to be clarified. Either the arts are passively dependent on social reality, a proposition which I take to be that of mechanical materialism, or a vulgar misinterpretation of Marx. Or the arts, as the creators of consciousness, determine social reality, the proposition which the Romantic poets sometimes advance. Or finally, the arts, while ultimately dependent, with everything else, on the real economic structure, operate in part to reflect this structure and its consequent reality, and in part, by affecting attitudes towards reality, to help *or hinder* the constant business of changing it. I find Marxist theories of culture confused because they seem to me, on different occasions and in different writers, to make use of all these propositions as the need serves.[7]

Writing this in 1958, Williams had not yet discovered the Frankfurt school, which would become a focus of his study in later years.[8] He defined his position against three possible methodological preoccupations in the field of cultural studies. The first, which he called "mechanical materialism," derived cultural processes (the formations of the individual and collective conscience) from the "reality" of social relations. While perhaps *reductionist* in its emphasis, this position takes cultural productions to be the effects of a reality that these cultural productions can only represent in a merely adequate way. For Williams, the resurgence of a reflexive theory in cultural studies denies works of art their autonomy, their intrinsic complexity, and their role in the reproduction of the social world. Access to reality is always already informed by our representations of it, and to judge the quality of a work's depiction of reality, we must first acknowledge the role of works of art in the production of the categories that allow us to perceive this reality. Inversely, the second position, which is *idealist*, attributes to the artist's work the capacity to produce the social world in its entirety. This description of the "poet as legislator" brings out an apparent contradiction between

---

7   Raymond Williams, *Culture and Society: 1780–1950* (New York: Anchor, 1959), 292–3.

8   See the third chapter of Jones, *Raymond Williams's Sociology*, 61–91.

(vulgar) Marxism and Romanticism.[9] While the first would conceptualize a signifier as the transparent conduit of a signified, the second would grant to cultural formations the ability to make the sum total of all social phenomena. The Romantic attitude, when defined in this way, is as unilateral as the mechanical materialist position, if under a different banner: it denies the existence of economic relations that organize the social world and condition cultural forms.

Williams tried to resolve this apparent contradiction by the formulation of a program of cultural studies that, holding tight to the Marxist position, recognized how economy is the dominant determining factor for all spheres of social life but that claimed, in keeping with a Romantic ideal, the role of cultural affects in the transformation of social reality. Michael Löwy and Robert Sayre are right to say that Williams exceeded the opposition between Marxism and Romanticism, citing how poetry furnished for him the basis of a moral critique against industrial modernity.[10] By Williams's time, the use of naturalist motifs in the critique of modernity had already become current in English socialism, as attested to in the proto-ecological critique of industrial society by William Morris (1834–1896), for whom Williams had a great appreciation.[11] But, for Williams, the rebirth of a Romantic spirit was not intended simply to breathe new life into utopian themes.

He found in English Romanticism the formation of an epistemology of cultural critique. The revolutionary Romantic poet was at once a utopian dreamer who claimed to have found the possibility for a desirable future in a past social world, and a producer who supported the role of art in the transformation of the present. Williams also studied cultural formations that allow us to imagine the practical sense of a revolution of the actual. For example, "with unusual precision, what we can later call a Romantic structure of feelings" appeared in the pastoral forms of the

9   Williams, *Culture and Society*, 292.

10   Michael Löwy and Robert Sayre, "Le courant romantique dans les sciences sociales en Angleterre: Edward P. Thompson et Raymond Williams," *L'Homme et la Société* 110 (1993): 56.

11   Williams, *Culture and Society*, 140.

eighteenth century.[12] For Williams, economic reality is determinative, but it's informed by immanent cultural processes.

The relation between economic reality and cultural formations needs some clarification. In *The Politics of Style*, Daniel Hartley proposes that we think of this conjunction according to a "principle of immanence." In response to Williams, he writes that "[there] is no way of constructing a relation between 'literature' and 'society' because without literature the society is not actual. Literature is immanent to society, a constitutive force within it."[13] The provocative statement that society is not real without literature holds for all cultural processes, as long as they are signifying. It means several things. First, it insists on the role of literature in the construction of society. It follows that the study of social phenomena is "concrete" only if we pay attention to their immanent significations. Cultural processes are not only the *form* of the appearance of a social reality that constructs human action; to the extent that culture marks the whole of signifying systems, culture is a constitutive aspect of all social processes, including economic ones. In Williams's lexicon, this "integrated conscience" is at play in all sorts of activities, whether manual or intellectual.[14] Categories that help us think about the real—culture, society, nature—do not demarcate ontological space in the world, but they have a role in shaping practice. Categories give meaning to practices without which they would not be able to be undertaken, realized, or interpreted—without which they simply would not exist. The most striking example is that of language, which is "practical consciousness—a constitutive element of all activity and an indissoluble element of all human self-formation."[15] No intervention in nature exists outside of language's meanings and the values we lend to nature. The proximity of this work to socially engaged practices taking place at the same time in Marxist anthropology (in the work of Maurice Godelier, for example) is

---

12 Williams, *The Country and the City*, 79.
13 Daniel Hartley, *The Politics of Style: Towards a Marxist Poetics* (Boston: Brill, 2017), 115.
14 Raymond Williams, *What I Came to Say* (London: Radius, 1989), 204.
15 Hartley, *The Politics of Style*, 108.

not happenstance:[16] it bears witness to the time's concern with leaving behind economic reductionism and reinvesting a social efficacy into symbolic forms that certain Marxist practitioners had denied them. However, the point for Williams was not to compare our societies to non-capitalist ones so we can understand them better, but to come up with a critique of the social world on the basis of its immanent meanings. This is different from the project of anthropologists. The "sociology of forms" that defines the later work of Williams is a study of social phenomena—social "reality"—through cultural productions.[17] It's in this context that a specific analysis of the representations of nature takes on its full meaning.

In a paper from 1971 called "Ideas of Nature," Williams states that our understanding of nature was always already socialized by a language encoded with the relations of production: "It is very significant that most of the terms we have used in this relationship—the conquest of nature, the domination of nature, the exploitation of nature—are derived from the real human practices: relations between men and men."[18]

His words seem to indicate that social relations between humans precede relations to nature between humans and nonhumans. The conquest, domination, and exploitation of nature would be the effects of power relations between people. But, in reality, his text is about the "idea" of nature and ways of describing it. In short, it argues that our experiences of nature are always already socialized by language, and that representations are configured by vocabularies and grammars that organize the real in different ways. Accessing the logic of the real is only possible through linguistic mediations produced within social relations. We cannot turn a blind eye to the possibility that our relations with nature are purely anthropomorphic projections of human relations onto natural exteriority: intending to talk about nature, we might only be really talking about society. We imagine relating to nature in the same

---

16   Maurice Godelier, *The Mental and the Material: Thought Economy and Society* (London: Verso, 2012).

17   Raymond Williams, *The Sociology of Culture* (Chicago: University of Chicago Press, 1995), 143.

18   Williams, "Ideas of Nature," 84.

way that we relate to everything in the human world. Williams looks for
the causes of this anthropomorphism:

> If we say only that we have mixed our labor with the earth, our forces
> with its forces, we are stopping short of the truth that we have done
> this unequally: that for the miner and the writer the mixing is differ-
> ent, though in both cases real; and that for the laborer and the man
> who manages this labor, the producer and the dealer in his products,
> the difference is wider again. Out of the ways in which we have inter-
> acted with the physical world we have made not only human nature
> and an altered natural order; we have also made societies.[19]

Williams was writing about the naturalist consequences of historical
materialism: while societies are transformed through acting on their
environment, it's essential to recognize the role of how we relate to nature
as an element of social history. Human organizations emerge and develop
based on constant interactions in their environment. The production of
human natures presupposes an actualization of subjective potentials by
practices that relate to the physical world in different ways. However, the
physical world and social practices share a common structure, since they
are interactive forces. Williams did not, of course, think of climatic
examples, but the increase in tornadoes and hurricanes linked to global
warming is very much the sign of an intermingling of physical human
and nonhuman forces. The production of greenhouse gases is the result
of technological activity that modifies the underlying conditions of a
certain number of meteorological phenomena. But, as Williams points
out, this entanglement between human labor and natural productivity is
done in a very unequal manner.

Humans produce their living conditions based on the conditions of
the physical world. Little by little, social relations are cemented in place
based on different uses of nature. Williams's examples allow us to state
the point more precisely: the writer and the miner, but especially "the
laborer and the man who manages this labor," do not have the same

---

19   Ibid.

relation to nature.[20] We can immediately see the masculine, modern character of the productive labor tropes that William invokes; then, the domestic or reproductive laborer establishes links between human labor and natural potentials in other ways that are absent here. The miner modifies his environment by the extraction of a part of nature through an intense activity; he develops his physical potential through the acquisition of the technical skill of handling tools and machines. The writer hardly modifies his material environment at all, and his physical exercise is limited to little more than what energy is expended on writing and its technologies. In this case, the human nature that is produced is linked to the writer's body and physical means. But, admittedly, these individual practices are not reducible to subjective characters; they are the result of social relations. The writer benefits from having money (from public or private means, founded on productivity, salary, or profit) that allows devotion to "unproductive" tasks while the miner earns a salary for extracting biophysical resources necessary for the production of goods. So relations to the natural environment depend on a social division of labor. Meanwhile, it's between "the laborer and the man who manages this labor" that the difference is the most evident.

There is a difference between the direct producer and the "man who manages the labor" only in a property system where the person who works the means of production does not own them. Effectively, the power of organizing labor presupposes that the laborer is working in compliance with the will of the person who owns the means of production and who modifies the labor process according to the logic of profit. Without this, the constraint exercised by the exploiters (appropriating the means of labor) does not pass through the organization of labor itself but through an "extra-economic" constraint—taxes, for example. Only dependence on the market and the appropriation of the means of production guarantee this deference to the will of the capitalist class. This "real subsumption" of the peasant laborer presupposes a previous dispossession of the principal object—the land. To wit, a specific relation

---

20   Ibid.

to the land determines class position in the social relation between producer (the salaried peasant) and the exploiter (the person who organizes labor). Relations to the land are conditioned by class relations that are themselves the products of the social history of the means of appropriating nature.

Williams's examples are typical for the modern era (the writer, the miner, the peasant, the producer, the merchant), but they rely more specifically on the class structure of English capitalism: they indicate, at once, a division between intellectual and manual laborers; a separation between direct producer and the holder of the means of production; and the distinction between the sphere of production and that of the circulation of value ("the producer and the merchant"). In each case, these examples propound masculine functions. Socially differentiated relations to the environment are effectively not only the results of a social history that would determine the places of each person in society before organizing particular ecological relations, but they also have contributed to the production of places, hierarchies, and power relations within collectivities. Agrarian capitalist class relations emerge due to an appropriation of the natural means of social reproduction.

According to Williams, while ideas of nature are reflections of the social world (domination, conquest, exploitation), this is true because the social world is born from our relations to nature (appropriation, depredation, pillage). This is what leads him to develop a theory of the socialization of nature by language (as a primary conditioning of experience) where the social emerges and develops based on relations to natural materiality. But such an imaginary is possible also because our experience of nature is translated into a mediatized language by cultural and literary forms.

The City and the Country: A Cultural History of Nature

Published in 1973, *The Country and the City* is Williams's most concerted attempt to think about the relation between nature and culture.[21] Briefly stated, the Welsh scholar traced a genealogy of the city and the country in English literature, which undercuts any sense of a stable relation between the two locations. He did not assume that these terms adequately identified the permanence of two separate realties, but he started from the idea that the evolution of the representations of the city and the country modifies the relations between nature and culture.

In Williams's book, there is a commentary on the cultural forms that emerge in English literature, and these forms bear witness across time to a renewed attachment to the land and an evolution of values associated with it:

> The detailed histories indicate everywhere that many old forms, old practices and old ways of feeling survived into periods in which the general direction of new development was clear and decisive. And then what seems an old order, a traditional society, keeps appearing, reappearing, at bewilderingly various dates: in practice as an idea, to some extent based in experience, against which contemporary change can be measured. The structure of feeling within which this backward reference is to be understood is then not primarily a matter of histori-cal explanation and analysis. What is really significant is this particu-lar kind of reaction to the fact of change, and this has more real and more interesting social causes.[22]

Williams's project was to evaluate the meaning of the return of old forms in a period transitioning to capitalism. At the moment when "capitalist agriculture . . . was being successfully pioneered," classical

---

21   For Daniel Hartley, the two principles that allow us to explain Williams's work are the concepts of immanence and complexity. See, most importantly, Daniel Hartley, "On Raymond Williams: Complexity, Immanence, and the Long Revolution," *Meditations* 30, no. 1 (Spring 2016): 46.

22   Williams, *The Country and the City*, 35.

themes (the pastoral, for example) were reinvested with new values based on the celebration of a feudal and aristocratic order more "natural" and more "organic" than capitalism.[23] What is being measured is the reaction to the historical change indexed through representations of nature. Williams noted that neopastoral metaphors of the seventeenth century reanimated the Virgilian pastoral while profoundly changing its meaning.

As Virgil's *Georgics* expressed a tension between "the pleasures of rural settlement and the threat of loss and eviction," so too the English neopastoral expressed a conflict between the country apology and the fear of being uprooted.[24] But it was the city that would incite fear in the future. Whether praising rural life or execrating the transformations taking place there, the neopastoral poets rendered the city the origin of everything bad. In each and every case, rural life and its economic and social relations are idealized. Williams writes, "More deeply, however, in a conventional association of Christian and classical myth, the provident land is seen as Eden."[25] This idealization is produced according to two distinct modalities through which it extols an ancient natural order in desuetude marked by peasant suffering, or, conversely, it grants a particular value to the recent development of capitalism. The principal innovation of the neopastoral is situating poems at the heart of the manor, the new center of agrarian capitalist power.

Williams was worried about uprooting this remnant of the past from its Romantic idealization: whether this took the form of criticism of the new order, as in the work of Oliver Goldsmith (1728–1774), or a favorable opinion, as that expressed by Abraham Cowley (1618–1667). Thus, it was possible to trace a history of criticism from the poet George Crabbe (1754–1832) to the Irish writer Oliver Goldsmith in *The Village* (1783). Crabbe denounced the paradisical vision of a traditional rural community integrated into an eternal natural order:

---

23   Ibid., 35–6.
24   Ibid., 17.
25   Ibid., 31.

I grant indeed that fields and flocks have charms
For him that grazes or for him that farms;
But when amid such pleasing scenes I trace
The poor laborious natives of the place,
And see the mid-day sun, with fervid ray,
On their bare heads and dewy temples play;
While some, with feebler heads and fainter hearts,
Deplore their fortune, yet sustain their parts,
Then shall I dare these real ills to hide
In tinsel trappings of poetic pride?[26]

In this poem, Crabbe criticized an idyllic vision of the English country-side and its specific form in neopastoral literature. Instead, he wished to show how working the land had always been a difficult job, due to erosion of soil quality, the whims of the weather, and the exploited life of peasants. In other words, while it was necessary to criticize how the peasants were dispossessed of their land, leading to the collapse of rural communities, this criticism was not offered to suggest that we revert to a mythical natural past. That was the meaning of the question in this section of the poem. For Williams, the question concerned the place of the poet in a world under violent attack, where "habits, institutions, and experiences clash" leading to a "crisis of perspective."[27] In line with Crabbe, Williams would always be suspicious of idealized forms of an ancient order in harmony with nature. This idealization only masked the difficulty of peasant life and its violent exploitation. The difficulty for this line of criticism lay in showing how the situation could get worse with agrarian capitalism without idealizing the preceding state of affairs: "In many thousands of cases, there is more community in the modern village, as a result of this process of new legal and democratic rights, than at any point in the recorded or imagined past."[28]

---

26   George Crabbe, *The Village: A Poem. In Two Books. By the Revd. George Crabbe, Chaplain to his grace the Duke of Rutland* (London: J. Dodsley, Pall-Mall, 1783), 4.

27   Williams, *The Country and the City*, 20.

28   Ibid., 104.

The myth of old rural England—and the encomiums about its peren-
nity or the eulogies about its disappearance—was a cultural form emerging from the agrarian capitalist transition where Williams found the
traces of residual forms of a rural critique of industrial modernity. The
idea of an "organic" or "natural" society is often accompanied by a
critique of the morality of the city, seen as the place where the ancient
ways are broken down by industrial society. Williams argued unstint-
ingly for the idea that capitalism was born in a countryside deep in the
grips of misery and exploitation. The profoundly rural dimension of
capitalism, the difficulty of the peasant life that preceded it, and the
contradictory tendencies of the city were masked by "romantic
anti-urbanism":[29]

> Yet there is a sense in which the idea of the enclosures, localized to just
> that period in which the Industrial Revolution was beginning, can
> shift our attention from the real history and become an element of that
> very powerful myth of modern England in which the transition from
> a rural to an industrial society is seen as a kind of fall, the true cause
> and origin of our social suffering and disorder. It is difficult to over-
> estimate the importance of this myth, in modern social thought. It is a
> main source for the structure of feeling which we began by examining:
> the perpetual retrospect to an "organic" or "natural" society. But it is
> also a main source for that last protecting illusion in the crisis of our
> own time: that it is not capitalism which is injuring us, but the more
> isolable, more evident system of urban industrialism. The questions
> involved are indeed very difficult, but for just this reason they require
> analysis, at each point and in each period in which an element of this
> structure can be seen in formation.[30]

Here, Williams's project was to identify historical moments when the
structure of experience occludes how capitalism causes suffering so as to
focus instead on a naturalist critique of urbanism. The ideal of a return

---

29   Ibid., 215.
30   Ibid., 96.

to natural, rural life is ambivalent. It brings up real suffering, namely, the fact of the separation with the natural conditions of life; but it also deflects the real causes of this suffering while proposing instead a moral critique of the city and industrialization. The myth of a rural harmony is, at once, a critical counterpoint necessary for modern life, and it is the sign of a masking of the material causes of real suffering.

Nevertheless, Williams tried to retain the utopian possibility of a direct experience of the land:

> The song of the land, the song of rural labor, the song of delight in . . . our physical world, is too important and too moving to be tamely given up, in an embittered betrayal, to the confident enemies of all significant and actual independence and renewal.[31]

In the end, the ability of these remnant cultural forms to support the project of emerging forms was what counted. In Hartley's reading, these are the first signs of Williams's new theoretical perspective on an ambivalent modernity where the valorization of the new is consistent with having chosen a cultural heritage, that is, having chosen a self-aware tradition.[32] The study of cultural forms is never aimed only at understanding the status and meaning of artistic works in their times but is always also aimed at unearthing their lasting relevance for new forms and understanding their effects in contemporary politics. While these artistic works are part of what is assumed to be the fabric of the past, they actually manage to retrospectively create new relations to the earth for ancestral societies. These new relations can then be realized in practice through inscribing them in the eternal present of tradition.

One of the seminal problems of this chapter lies here. How can the evolution of representations of the city and the country modify their real relations? How exactly has the evolution of cultural forms contributed to the transformation of the city and the country?

---

31   Ibid., 271.
32   Hartley, "On Raymond Williams," 51.

Literary Landscapes and the Production of the Real

One of the most striking examples in Williams's work concerns the invention of the English countryside through the trope of the *cottage*. The literary utopia of a countryside without labor and laborers, inherited from the neopastoralism of the seventeenth century (and illustrated by Ben Jonson's poem "To Penshurst" among others), was brought about by the landscapes and vistas designed by architects and manor landscape architects.[33] They built

> a rural landscape emptied of rural labor and of laborers; a sylvan and watery prospect, with a hundred analogies in neopastoral painting and poetry, from which the facts of production had been banished: the roads and approaches artfully concealed by trees, so that the very fact of communication could be visually suppressed; inconvenient barns and mills cleared away out of sight . . . avenues opening to the distant hills, where no details disturbed the general view; and this landscape seen from above, from the new elevated sites.[34]

The entire countryside landscape was redesigned from the view offered by the high manor windows; this was the new locus of "control and command."[35] As society transitioned to capitalism, a new literature arose from the expropriation of the peasantry and *enclosures* that arose in this environment where all social relations were being profoundly disturbed, and this literature made the countryside an ideal and a problem: an ideal in the sense of a harmonious life inherited from the mythic past, and a problem from the point of view of a world founded on labor and exploitation. What poetry and the novel attempted to resolve by the metaphor of harmony, the large landowners and English capitalists resolved by the production of a new idea of

---

33 Ben Jonson, "To Penshurst" (1616), in *Ben Jonson: Poems*, ed. Thom Gunn (London: Faber, 2005), 66–8.

34 Williams, *The Country and the City*, 125.

35 Ibid.

the rural, designed and lived according to the norms of this very liter-ature. "This is an alteration of landscape, by an alteration of seeing," Williams concludes.[36]

Yet Williams never intended to reduce the production of landscape to a simple materialization of some type of ideal contents. Changes of liter-ary forms bear witness to the attempt to resolve problems that not only implicate individual authors but literature in general, and can be linked to a "real social history."[37] It was not only a new landscape that was invented but the very idea of landscape itself:

> A working country is hardly ever a landscape. The very idea of land-scape implies separation and observation. It is possible and useful to trace the internal histories of landscape painting, landscape writing, landscape gardening and landscape architecture, but in any final anal-ysis we must relate these histories to the common history of a land and its society.[38]

The idea of landscape is reliant on the possibility of contemplation by an observer situated outside of the landscape (the vista of a capitalist lord contemplating his domain through his grand manor windows). In its aesthetic forms and practical realizations, landscape only appears after the "separation" of the observer from that which is observed, of the indi-vidual from the land. The landscape is born from the disjunction between aesthetics and pragmatism, which Williams considered, in the end, to be the result of a "separation of production and consumption."[39] The aesthetic consumption of landscape (contemplation) is an effect of the capitalist consumption of the fruits of the land produced by producers excluded from the landscape itself. Landscape is the empirical cultural form of the destruction of the "working country" and the image of the separation of labor and land. To be meaningful, disciplinary

---

36   Ibid., 87.
37   Williams, *Problems in Materialism and Culture*, 26.
38   Williams, *The Country and the City*, 120.
39   Ibid., 121.

histories—in literature, painting, landscape architecture, and architecture—must be tied to the social history that allows these disciplines to exist in the first place. It is impossible to imagine the seventeenth-century English countryside without the eviction of the peasantry, but it's equally impossible to understand this expropriation without the narratives that traced its contemporaneity and that made sense of it. This "structure of feeling" is a fleeting phenomenon that does not mean anything outside of the communal history of the land and society in which it takes place. A new cultural relation to the land accompanies the changes in social relations, which are themselves transformations of a way of being and acting in nature.

To the extent that the landscape is a product of social history, it manifests political struggle through the question of the representational forms of the real. In Williams, representations are polysemous, just like the culture in which they are articulated: they mark at once individual works and general perception, seen as the result of a history of practices. Struggles for control of nature are born out in landscapes, each shaped by the material cultures of social classes. Each struggle mobilizes specific environmental values and meanings so as to realize the norms of their imaginary in the world. The difference between the ways of relating to nature and the form of their representation is the condition of possibility of a cultural productivity, that is to say, of its capacity to inform the world and transform it. We can speak of a "cultural naturalism" for this theory of the formal mediations of the social history of nature.

Cultural Naturalism and Encompassing Ways of Life

Williams's originality lies in the way that he linked the philosophical and literary meanings of the concept of naturalism. The idea that societies belong to their physical environment (in the philosophical sense) is inseparable from the history of the literary forms of naturalism, where nature is a silent protagonist. More precisely, the dramatic convention of the nineteenth century, which established the use of the concept of naturalism in literature, codified an emerging relation to natural materiality, where this materiality went from being a demiurgical power to a mute but omnipotent character. For Williams, the way that societies acted in nature and the social effect of the power of natural realities were always interpreted in the cultural forms that bore witness to a problem in social history. However, the emergence of this cultural naturalism was profoundly linked to the new representations of the city, and the way they modified the perception of the environment in general. At this juncture, it would be useful to delve into some literary narratives of the city in order to understand how a "cultural naturalism" is situated in Williams's work, and how this naturalism leads to the relativization of the centrality of production in the ecological future of societies.

Eighteenth-century England witnessed the transformation of both the countryside and London. The moral encoding of the city as a space of "waste and profligacy" runs alongside the pastoral myth of innocent nature.[40] Yet, Williams notes that "this moral view, of waste and profligacy, allows room not only for the contrast with innocent nature but also with civilized industry. The celebration of production, which had embraced the land, now extends to the city."[41] Criticism of modern urbanism opens the door to a celebration of "industrial civilization" that will lead to a city entirely given over to production. Just as London was welcoming all the chaff of England—landless peasants, wandering vagabonds, and unemployed domestic laborers—the city was being reconstructed on the model of the manor, and it became a power center of English capitalism. The endless labyrinths of working-class neighborhoods contrasted with "the building of town mansions, the laying out of squares and fashionable terraces: the 'Georgian' London now so often abstracted."[42] Architecture forms conceived of in the feudal countryside were repatriated to the city where they were called on to play a similar role: control the dangerous masses, give form to power, and command the city's productive means in the future. The confusion between city and industry—which results from the project of transforming the city

---

40   Ibid., 143.
41   Ibid.
42   Ibid., 145.

into a locus of pure production—leads to the emergence of a "romantic anti-urbanism," whose best examples can be found in Charles Dickens and in Engels's *The Condition of the Working Class in England*.[43] The irony of the situation is clearly visible: the city is transformed according to cultural codes that previously led to the disruption of the countryside. In *Dombey and Sons*, Dickens launched into a moral critique of the city based on its varieties of pollution:

> Alas! . . . Breathe the polluted air, foul with every impurity that is poisonous to health and life; and have every sense, conferred upon our race for its delight and happiness, offended, sickened and disgusted, and made a channel by which misery and death alone can enter. Vainly attempt to think of any simple plant, or flower, or a wholesome weed, that, set in this foetid bed, could have its natural growth, or put its little leaves forth to the sun as God designed it. And then, calling up some ghastly child, with stunted form and wicked face, hold forth on its unnatural sinfulness, and lament its being, so early, far away from Heaven—but think a little of its having been conceived, and born, and bred, in Hell![44]

Two concepts of nature are evident in this passage. First, nature is the ultimate criterion for moral judgement. We can evaluate the morality of individuals and societies according to the ways that they respect or not the universal natural order, which is the basis for a certain idea of justice. Second, industrial society has produced an environment where "there [are] so few things in the world about us, most unnatural, and yet most natural in being so!"[45] So, a second material nature determines individual behavior. This passage clearly articulates the problem of naturalist moral philosophy in the modern era. Since nature was transformed such that the worst human products are now natural objects (or "first nature"), how

---

43   Friedrich Engels, *The Condition of the Working Class in England* (1845), trans. Florence K. Wischnewetzky (New York: John C. Lovell, 1887).

44   Charles Dickens, *Dombey and Sons* (London: Bradbury & Evans, 1848), 459.

45   Ibid.

are we to judge Dickens's literary character against the nature of practices? Since material nature can no longer furnish the criteria of justice
and injustice, what can be used to make moral judgments?

The character of the dishonest and naughty child is one of the most
common in Dickens. Everywhere in Dickens, we find these typically
impoverished characters whose subjectivities were produced by an
immoral environment. There would be, then, different human natures
depending upon the environments that have shaped them.
Environments—a concept that is both ecological and social—produce
characters whose morality we can judge at the onset by the norms of the
context itself. However, according to Dickens, this environmental
production of human natures does not prevent us from holding to a
universal natural morality that would transcend class. To the contrary,
human natures, seen as historical products of singular environments,
enter into contradiction with the moral ideal of a universal nature by
which we can judge the perversion of the city.

What takes place in this passage, then, is the appearance of a new
"structure of feeling" where Romanticism, which celebrated the virtues
of eternal nature, is brought into conflict with a nascent naturalism. The
image of this "black and dense cloud" speaks not only to the ecological
and moral effects of urbanization but also to the end of a poetics founded
on the idealization of nature as a utopian norm.[46] In this passage, the
parallel established between the impossibility of the growth of plants in
a fetid environment and the sickness of children raised against nature is
the sign of how human beings belong to their environment. Once and
for all, nature, still thought of as the *moral* criteria of action (Romanticism)
has been so transformed that it now *determines* the social and physical
conditions of practice (naturalism). The material degradation of nature,
which bears witness to an alienated industrial civilization, prevents
action and moral judgement. It modifies the values and the judgements
that we can use in the social world, and it imposes new cultural forms.
The Romantic image of the subjectivity of the creator who is being torn
from the world through a leap into mythical nature enters into conflict

---

46   Williams, *The Country and the City*, 156.

with the representation of a degraded environment that no longer offers any means of action but rather predetermines human behavior.[47] In this passage, Dickens dramatizes the tension between a residual form of Romanticism and "pre-emergent" naturalism.[48]

Dickens is not a naturalist author in the sense the term was understood at the end of the nineteenth century. But in his work there is a "structure of feeling" that is naturalist, an emergent form of "social experiences in solution."[49] Through his concept of a structure of feeling, Williams wants to capture elements of social life in evolution, "irreducible to pre-existent ('precipitated') modes of thought or representations."[50] He says that they would be called "structures of *experiences*," if this term did not otherwise bring up the idea of a way of thinking dependent on past practices. To capture this flux of representations and novel emotions, we must understand their "structure," or their "specific internal relations," that is to say, their historical processuality and their social meaning.[51] In *Drama from Ibsen to Brecht*, Williams studied the transformation of this naturalist structure of feeling into a formal problem related to conventions, typical of the theater at the end of the nineteenth century and the beginning of the twentieth century:

> In any precise analysis of the [naturalist] structure and its conventions, a particular relation between men and their environment is evidently assumed. If we see, in its detail, the environment men have created, we shall learn the truth about them.[52]

For naturalism, the problem of form is linked to the problematic experience of living in a world where the environment (transformed by societies) shapes individuals in a lasting way. The environment is both the

---

47   Löwy and Sayre, "Raymond Williams," 75–91.
48   Williams, *Marxism and Literature*, 126, 132.
49   Ibid., 133.
50   Hartley, "On Raymond Williams," 42.
51   Williams, *Marxism and Literature*, 132.
52   Raymond Williams, *Drama from Ibsen to Brecht* (New York: Oxford University Press, 1969), 335.

historical product that expresses the nature of social relations and the milieu that shapes human subjectivities. Literary form must, then, acknowledge the loss of human freedom in the face of the environment's power to act. That is why the social and material context becomes a "character" important to the fictional drama and why "naturalism actually used speech less than most other dramatic forms."[53] In 1978, Williams differentiated between the structures of naturalist and realist feelings while giving the second a more dynamic dimension. While naturalism "traps" characters in an environment from which they cannot escape, realism insists on the "possibility of intervention to change them."[54] These structures of feelings explain how new political orientations emerge. Effectively, we can understand human societies by studying the effects of their production system on the physical environment. This reformulates historical materialism. Different from orthodox, or vulgar, historical materialism, what Williams proposed gives a central place to the cultural "mediations" through which we gain access to a type of nature that we transform in the process.

To the extent that "men [are] accustomed to seeing their immediate environment through received intellectual and literary forms," aesthetic production is a decisive element in the modification of the environment itself.[55] Culture is a productive process within the social. It defines production in toto as being mediatized by inherited meanings and as being "specific practices, of 'arts,' as social uses of material means of production."[56] Williams gives several examples of such practices: "from language as material 'practical consciousness' to specific technologies of writing and forms of writing, through to mechanical and electronic communications systems."[57] The study of culture as a productive process defines the general project of Williams's "cultural materialism." In short, he proposes two epistemological ideas: (a) we *understand* societies based on the way they produce their environment on the material as well as the

---

53   Williams, "Realism," 2, 5.
54   Ibid., 5.
55   Williams, *The Country and the City*, 142.
56   Williams, *Problems in Materialism and Culture*, 243.
57   Ibid.

cultural levels; (b) we must study culture as a productive process of meanings and evaluations that modify social relations to nature.

However, we can recognize in these two epistemological propositions the position of a "cultural naturalism" built on Williams's model of cultural materialism: social beings transform their physical environment through applying the values of many aesthetic factors. The ways that societies relate to nature are therefore simultaneously shaped by material productions and cultural formations. The latter inform the former, and cultural formations give material productions meaning and sketch out the contours of a present that toggles between the inherited forms of the past and the emerging forms of the future. Williams's point is not so much about a world split between social practices and cultural representations as it is about a historical universe where culture is immanent in the social. On this point, *The Country and the City* is not directly about "nature" and "culture," but rather it investigates the literary form that this distinction took on during the era of primitive accumulation in England (town and country). We can also take from his cultural naturalism an epistemological argument about the experience of nature itself: it never takes place outside the cultural forms that provide its meaning and the values that contribute to its transformation.[58] Yet, the assimilation of culture within a process as productive as the "economy"—which is immanent within it, disturbs it, renders it more complex, and outstrips it—leaves no room to question the concept of production in the definition in the social world.

Production and Life

Paradoxically, his study of the productive dimension of culture led Williams to relativize the centrality of economic production in the social world. In the conclusion to *Towards 2000*, he tries to determine the meaning of

---

58   One of the epistemological stances of this cultural naturalism is the outdated nature of the theoretical distinction between "base" and "superstructure." See, in particular, Williams, *Marxism and Literature*, 75–82.

ecological movements in terms of theory and politics.[59] Following the path that he had begun to sketch out in *Marxism and Literature* (1977), he sets Marx's concept of a mode of production against that of a whole way of life.[60] Williams recognizes the critical value of this Marxist concept in the study of capitalism, but he rejects its centrality in historical materialism:

> The concept of a "mode of production" has been a major explanatory element of the dominant social orders through which we have been living. It has enabled us to understand many stages of our social and material history, showing that the central ways in which production is organized have major and changing effects on the ways in which we relate to each other and learn to see the world. But what has now to be observed is that the concept itself is at some important points a prisoner of the social orders which it is offering to analyze. It has been most successful and enlightening in its analysis of capitalism, and this is not accidental, for in its own conceptual form it seized the decisive element of capitalism: that this is a mode of production which comes to dominate both society as a whole and—which is less often stressed—the physical world. The eventual inadequacy of the concept is then that it has selected a particular historical and material orientation as essential and permanent.[61]

To the extent that capitalism is an economic system in which production leads to the accumulation of profit for the intermediary of the commodity's sale on the market, it tends to subsume all forms of life (human and nonhuman) under the logic of the accumulation of value. Thus, production is the principal form of "intervention" of *capitalist* societies in nature.[62] Yet, Williams had grave doubts about its centrality in premodern eras and non-modern societies. Moreover, he believed that this concept does not let us "see beyond" capitalism.[63] In Marxism,

---

59   Raymond Williams, *Towards 2000* (New York: Penguin, 1985).
60   Williams, *Marxism and Literature*, 300.
61   Williams, *Towards 2000*, 263–4.
62   Ibid., 265.
63   Ibid., 264.

skepticism about the centrality of production is based on a historical problem and a strategic question.

Historically speaking, production can no longer be thought of as the principal form of intervention in nature. Williams was adamant that during the Neolithic Revolution, appropriation and production became essential forms of social activity in the physical world, without becoming the exclusive form of human interaction with the environment. In production, the means and object of labor become "raw materials" that can and must be appropriated to permit the transformation of nature.[64] Williams did not deny the necessity of this "orientation," that is to say, this form of "intervention" in the physical world. But he believed capitalism to be the sole mode of production in which this intervention is systematized and spread over all environmental and intersubjective relations. Effectively, to the extent that to produce means to appropriate and to transform a natural resource, production always holds the existence of this appropriable and transformable resource as a presumption of its activity. Production transforms the environment and labor into a raw material of activity, without which activity itself would be impossible. From this point of view, the fundamental power of capitalism is to have erected this necessary but specific form of intervention in nature as a universal and hegemonic form of relation. The "capture" of powerful technologies by a "class which defined its whole relationship to the world as one of appropriation" engenders a world in which "there is nothing but raw material: in the earth, in other people, and finally in the self."[65] Marx would remain a prisoner to the capitalist categories that he criticized. Considering the history of societies as a history of modes of production, he overemphasized the productive turn of capitalism. To put things simply, all ways of life are not reducible to modes of production; only capitalism is, properly speaking, a mode of production. And this "abstraction of production" has strategic consequences.[66]

---

64 Ibid., 61.
65 Ibid., 262.
66 Ibid., 264.

Politically speaking, then, Williams believed that any new form of historical materialism could not hope for the advent of a new mode of production, but that it should hope instead for the realization of a new way of life founded on other types of interventions in nature that are more respectful of nonhumans and individuals:

> Thus there are profound interconnections in the whole process of production—that version of relations with others and with the physical world—to which the now dominant social orders have committed themselves. The way forward is in the neglected, often repressed but still surviving alternative, which includes many conscious interventions in a constituted nature but which selects and directs these by a fundamental sense of the necessary connections with nature and of these connections as interactive and dynamic.[67]

Pragmatic critique of the destructive effects of capitalism could only lead to the realization of a naturalist way of life where interventions in the physical world were guided by the sense of our belonging and love for the earth. So, in proposing to substitute the concept of a whole way of life for the concept of the mode of production, Williams was trying to fuse the economic processes that determine the social world to the cultural forms in which they are present. In 1977, he wrote that since a mode of production always exists "within an existing culture" and since "all elements of social reality are interdependent ... Marxists should logically use the concept of 'culture' to mean a way of life in its totality, a general social process."[68] The concept of a mode of production has two weaknesses. First, it tends to mask the role of cultural mediations in our relation to the facts of nature. Second, it contributes to the reproduction of alienated relations while making production the heart of all social and ecological interactions. Relative to the new concept of the way of life *taken as a whole*, culture is naturalist, because only through it can we orient the actions of individuals and groups based upon their

---

67   Ibid., 263.
68   Williams, *Marxism and Literature*, 300–1.

fundamental belonging to the earth. If naturalism defines a way of being in the world, naturalist politics must allow us to live out less alienated relations with natures. An argument for a whole way of life that takes into consideration the belonging of humans to the earth forces us to turn away from the Promethean myth of production just as much as the myth of the natural harmony of the countryside.

As Hartley remarks, a preference for the broad but "vague" concept of a "way of life" over that of a *mode of production* allows us to integrate the silenced voices of modern society into a critique of capitalism and the possibility of its obsolescence.[69] Pacificist movements, ecology, and feminisms are not reducible to production mechanisms because, most often, they manage to fend it off. That fact that market logic does not assign them any value is proof of their "revolutionary character" and their capacity to propose other "ways of life" and means of subsistence.[70] These movements incarnate a new "structure of feeling" by which production is only one form of interacting with nature among others. Culture becomes a production of the sensible. As a collection of practices of meanings immanent within the social, it becomes a strategic place for political action.

The meaning of aesthetic motifs is never easy to circumscribe. A Romantic landscape can both give birth to a painting critical of modern life and idealize a mythical nature where all forms of relation have been effaced. Yet, today, we participate in the reinvention of material cultures that take into consideration the idea of our belonging to the land. What will these new cultures mean for us? Is this process no more than the resurgence of the reactionary motif of the community's ownership over the nation's eternal landscapes, or can we find in these movements the ideal of a harmonious community fighting against our estrangement from the world?

---

69   Hartley, "On Raymond Williams," 53.
70   Ibid.; Williams, *Towards 2000*, 262.

Taking Back the Land: The Practical Naturalism of José Carlos Mariátegui

Driving in the large luxurious American car that never ceased to remind him at such times of a boat; a boat manned by Dirk Burnaby himself, on the River Styx. He would drive, drive. He would not sleep. East of Luna Park, away from The Falls and into the interior. Something drew him like a magnet. It wasn't the woman but something nameless. The lewdly winking teasing lights of Dow Chemical, Carborundum, OxyChem, Swann Chemicals, Alliance Oil Refinery, Allied Steel. Pale smoke like drifting bandages. And fog. And mist, obscuring the moonlit sky. East Niagara Falls was a region of perpetual drizzle. Smells that had become visible. Rotted eggs, sour and sweet and yet astringent like disinfectant. A taste of ether. Dirk drove, fascinated. He guessed that he must be driving in the vicinity of Love Canal.

—Joyce Carol Oates, *The Falls*

The return of the land as a subject in the social sciences is accompanied by a "return to the land" in environmental ethics. In the context of climate change brought on by fossil capitalism, rural and communal agrarian lands are now viewed as places for the invention of less alienated ways of living. Yet these transformative practices are always historically situated, and their meaning is never the same. Between the position of Henry David Thoreau, who took to the wilderness in order to find the expression of the intrinsic naturalness of beings, and reinvestments in urban agriculture meant to satisfy the food needs of postindustrial cities of late capitalism, like Detroit in the 2000s, the gap is so vast that we cannot assign a universal, abstract meaning to the trope of "return to the land."[1] To be sure, its political meaning is ambiguous.

On the one hand, the return to the land bears witness to a practice critical of modernity and to an effort to limit the disruptions that it provokes in the metabolism of societies and environments. It's true that the countryside often provides an example of social life that is less separated from the natural conditions of reproduction, and so a life that has something about it that is more "authentic," in the sense that it's directly tied to the material bases of human existence. But, on the other hand, this return to the land is sometimes motivated by the desire to rediscover the original unity of humans and nonhumans in the reassuring stability of an eternal cosmos. In this case, it can lead to defining community through identitarian forms where "roots" become political in their stance against the "nomadism" of people in migratory circumstances.[2] We see, then, how the return to the land can lead directly to an ethnonationalist claim on the land.

These identitarian reactions to the ecological catastrophe facing us idealize the existence of a purportedly authentic nature. Whether as parts of certain American trends toward "bioregionalism," or in the

---

1   This is the position of Paula Dolci and Coline Perrin in their study of Sardinia's new wave of farmers after the economic crisis of 2008: "Retourner à la terre en Sardaigne, crises et installations en agriculture," *Tracés: Revue des sciences humaines* 33 (2017): 145–67.

2   It is impossible not to notice the ideology that subtends the platform of the National Rally, a French far-right political party, for the European elections in 2019. Taking up the distinction between "nomadism" and "rootedness," this program sets the "globalization" of elites and refugees off against the "localism" of European peoples: communitarianism, organic food, and so on. For a closer look at the phenomenon of "green nationalism," see Zoé Carle, "Contre-révolutions écologiques. Quand les droites dures investissent la défense de la nature," *Revue du Crieur* 8, no. 3 (2017): 44–61; or Andreas Malm and the Zetkin Collective, *White Skin, Black Fuel: On the Danger of Fossil Fascism* (London: Verso, 2021).

"green nationalism" of the ecologies of the French far right, these reactions are based on the logic of naturalism that contrasts the harmonious universe of societies and environments against a world in which capital exploits nature.[3] The intellectual investment in pointing out this separation goes hand in hand with a politics of "reconciliation."[4] Here, practical naturalism imagines the future as a return to a mythical past: displacement in space is accompanied by a new conception of time. In this cyclical chronology, the future allows the resolution of past antagonisms on the condition that it can return to enjoy the natural harmony of origins.[5] However, we know to what extent this periodization is incompatible with the anthropological and historical reality of the near infinite ways of that humans interact with nature. Relations to the environment have always presented a problem rather than proof: to assure the environmental conditions for social reproduction, it was always necessary to mobilize human powers and intelligences in various and often difficult natural contexts and in social groups in conflict. The relation between naturalism and the ideal of a return to the land gives rise to several difficulties.

First, there is the question of whether naturalism is necessarily linked to a mythology of origins where community is thought of as a harmonious bond of humans and nonhumans. If it is linked in this way to this primitive mythology, would that by itself be reason to abandon the idea? Could we not see in naturalism something else, namely, a utopian repertoire of revolutionary ecological practices? Is this eschatology of

3   Kirkpatrick Sale, *Dwellers in the Land: The Bioregional Vision* (San Francisco: Sierra Club Books, 1985).

4   The criticism of the idea of a "'reconciliation' with nature" runs throughout the collected works of Adorno and Horkheimer. See Max Horkheimer, *Eclipse of Reason* (New York: Oxford University Press, 1947); Max Horkheimer and Theodor W. Adorno, *Dialectic of Enlightenment*, trans. John Cumming (New York: Herder & Herder, 1972).

5   Michael Löwy and Robert Sayre developed the idea of a critical return to an original unity linking societies and nature in what they called the "contemporary Romanticism of Rousseauian sensibility." See Michael Löwy and Robert Sayre, *Romanticism Against the Tide of Modernity*, trans. Catherine Porter (Durham, NC: Duke University Press, 2002).

reconciliation founded solely on the erroneous assumption of an initial separation, or is its goal, from a practical point of view, to complicate the relation to nature in the crucible of the social world? Second, might we dispense with the question of whether the return to the land is progressive or reactionary, and focus instead on *which land* is meant when we make it the basis of non-disruptive social relations and the utopian norm of political praxis?[6] Is land the phenomenological ground on which all experience develops, or the materiality of agricultural labor? The heritage of a single piece of property, or the substrate of collective sovereignty? Third, must the return to the land speak about an identitarian definition of community (the belonging to a territory that is spatially circumscribed by the bonds of national bloodlines), or might it be the place of a reinvention of community based on the recognition of the multiple ways that we inhabit the earth?

The ambivalence of naturalism is a historical contradiction whose resolution will be political: forms of the idealization of natural life risk a Romantic racialization of the roots of community; inversely, by not using the critical terminology of naturalist motifs (in short, setting aside the concept of nature), we might lose track of the examples of domination written into the land. This is what historical materialism once understood. For certain strains of its thought, the uses and the appropriation of nature are determined by a history of conflicts where the peasantry plays a leading role. The metabolism of societies and environments is not a natural origin that humans perverted, and so it's not up to us to find it again; rather, it is a strategic objective that certain groups in conflict look to realize while collectively reappropriating the natural conditions of human existence. The belonging of societies to the land appears no longer as a presupposition but a result of a history of struggles for access to nature and its appropriation. I will talk about a "practical naturalism of peasant revolts" to provide examples of the unity that can arise through political activity.

---

6   Pierre Charbonnier, Bruno Latour, and Baptiste Morizot, "Redécouvrir la terre," *Tracés. Revue de Sciences humaines* 33 (2017): 227–52.

It's true that Marxism was, at first, an urban, worker movement, and that its main branches reflected this constituency. Nevertheless, Marxist traditions attentive to peasant struggles have also existed. All we have to do is think of the Marxist call for the "return of modern societies to a higher form of an 'archaic' type,"[7] or otherwise the sensibility for the "song of the land, the song of rural labor, [and] the song of delight with which we all share our physical world," as discussed in the work of Williams.[8] We can find other striking and original responses to environmental problems in the Peruvian Marxist thinker José Carlos Mariátegui. He attempted to invent a Peruvian path toward socialism based on the idea of a mythical past, an "Incan communism," where social relations were not founded on a class-based society or on the racial heritage of Spanish colonialism. The old way of relating to the earth was the sign of a different possible future, an egalitarian society that socialism could play its part in reviving. Of course, this imaginative representation of an agrarian Incan communism, which was heavily influenced by Engels's and Luxemburg's primitive communism, does not entirely correspond to historical reality. A myth of indigenous agrarian life plays the role in Mariátegui's materialist conception of history of a utopia that the politics of naturalism is meant to bring about. Here, the Peruvian thinker is exemplary in the way that he addresses the practical aspirations of the return to the land in a political philosophy that could end up being the future of communism.

Peasant War, Partisan Fight

In Marxism, the relation between the land and the peasantry is generally explained through historic, economic, and political means. Marxists are most interested in histories that mark the transition from feudalism to

---

7   See the first draft to Zasulich in Vera Zasulich and Karl Marx, "1881 Letters of Vera Zasulich and Karl Marx," trans. and ed. Teodor Shanin, *Journal of Peasant Studies* 45, no. 7 (2018): 1183–202.

8   Raymond Williams, *The Country and the City* (New York: Oxford University Press, 1975), 271.

capitalism. In terms of economics, Marxism studied class structure in agrarian communities, the modes of extracting ground rent, and the conjunctures with other domains of production.[9] Then, politically speaking, the problem was how to determine the revolutionary character of peasant struggles and the type of alliance that the urban proletariat could hope to have with the peasantry in the struggle to bring about the abolition of capital and the end of the state. Lenin and the Bolsheviks distrusted the supposedly conservative character of the peasantry, whose attachment to the land was the sign of a commitment to tradition. To them, even the most radical peasant struggles would have appeared to be old-fashioned skirmishes instead of the first uprisings of the great revolution itself.[10]

We know how important Engels's *The Peasant War in Germany* (1850) was in this regard. The mass peasant revolts that sent a shudder through Europe from 1517 to 1525—this final date marks when the armies of the Lutheran princes ended them for good at Frankenhausen—remain an important moment in revolutionary memory as they became a special means for conceptualizing peasant revolts in Marxism. Published several months after he joined the Baden Revolution, then taken up again and republished frequently until the end of his life, Engels's text played an essential role in the fleshing out of historical materialism. During this revolutionary campaign in Baden and Palatinate, Engels supported *manu militari* a democratic constitution for Germany. In *The Peasant War in Germany*, Engels was still thinking about the aborted revolution of 1848, which is the basis of the many parallels he pointed out. This text, published several years after *The Germany Ideology* (1844) and *The Communist Manifesto* (1848), claims to be one of the first illustrations of the Marxist concept of history. *The Class Struggles in France, 1848–1850*, Marx's book on the 1848 revolution, was published in 1850 as well.

9   See, in particular, Terence J. Byres, *Capitalism from Above and Capitalism from Below: An Essay in Comparative Political Economy* (Basingstoke: Macmillan, 1996), as well as Henry Bernstein, *Class Dynamics of Agrarian Change* (Halifax: Fernwood, 2010).

10   Eric Hobsbwam, *Primitive Rebels* (Manchester: Manchester University Press, 1959).

Basing his study of peasant revolts on the economic conditions of class struggle, Engels brought to the forefront a host of elements that cultural historians of the religious wars had ignored.[11]

For Engels, peasant rebellions announced the communist revolutions to come because they called for the end of private property. For nineteenth-century socialists, the writings of Thomas Müntzer (1489–1525), the theologian and the leader of the peasant uprising in Thuringia, provided an example of radical, universal equality. At a time when social relations were still largely feudal, the call for an end to private property was still too early, because only the proletariat—united through class—would have the power to bring it about. Müntzer's millenarianism bears witness to, according to Engels, the impossibility of overturning class structures due to the fact that the bourgeoisie had not yet come to power and the proletariat had not yet been formed into a revolutionary class. This is the reason why communism was still being expressed in a messianic language in the era of peasant uprisings. In Engels's book, three elements stand in contradiction: a revolutionary communism that can only be expressed through religious ideology (an anticipation of the future in mystical language); feudal relations of production that prevent the unity of the opposition (peasants, plebians, bourgeoises) around a common program in their struggles against feudal lords; and the rise of a bourgeois class looking to establish new property relations. To the extent that the movement was composed in no small part by a bourgeoisie looking not to abolish private property but to transform feudal property into capitalist property, it was impossible to accomplish a communist revolution, even if that was the implicit goal. To bring that about, there would have to be a near-complete opposition (or at least majority opposition) aimed at the conscious abolition of the privatization of the means of production.

The formulation of a proto-communist program at a time when the bourgeoisie did not yet have power is too much to ask for, but there were telltale signs of a new way of constructing social relations:

---

11   Friedrich Engels, *The Peasant War in Germany*, ed. Vic Schneierson, trans. unknown (1956; repr., Moscow: Progress Publishers, 1977).

This explains why the plebian opposition even then could not stop at fighting only feudalism and the privileged burghers; why, in fantasy at least, it reached beyond the then scarcely dawning modern bourgeois society . . . the chiliastic dream-visions of early Christianity offered a very convenient starting point. On the other hand, this sally beyond both the present and even the future could be nothing but violent and fantastic, and of necessity fell back within the narrow limits set by the contemporary situation at the very first practical application of it. The attack on private property and demand for common ownership was bound to resolve into a primitive organization of charity; vague Christian equality could at best resolve into civic "equality before the law" and elimination of all authority would finally culminate in the establishment of republican governments elected by the people. The anticipation of communism, nurtured by the imagination, became in reality an anticipation of modern bourgeois conditions.[12]

Engels believed that the failures of peasant revolutions were a foregone conclusion in a struggle where proto-communist ideology could not hope to make a dent in the structure of social relations in feudalism. To the extent that the peasant war anticipated forms of consciousness typical of future bourgeois societies, it could only have failed to radically transform a still-feudal society. Engels's "anachronistic" study of the peasant war does not make any unified statement about the nature of peasant movements in general.[13] Nevertheless, several of its elements would become influential on future Marxist studies on peasant struggles.

Communism is the movement for the abolition of the privatization of the means of production by a revolutionary class that fights against its exploitation. In all formations where the means of production belong to a single class, an owner class exploits the labor of direct producers. A

---

12   Ibid., 46.
13   For more reading on the subject of anachronisms in history, see Nicole Loraux, "Éloge de l'anachronisme en histoire," *Espaces Temps, Les Cahiers* 87/88 (2005): 127–39.

part of the produced wealth is extracted by those who own the means of production, or by those who possess political privileges that give them the right to (and the power over) them. It was only when the bourgeoisie took power by transforming feudal property into capitalist property that the opposition could gather around a common interest. Only when bourgeois political freedoms became universal could the struggle turn toward the relations of economic exploitation. In Engels's text—which is profoundly marked by the years 1848 to 1850—we see a certain historical mechanism: the communist revolution presupposes the development of capitalism. To the extent that bourgeois social relations (civil liberties and, especially, the right to capitalist private property) were not established in 1521–25, the peasant rebellions could not effectively overturn the social order on a large scale. They announced a bourgeois order more than a communist revolution.

Moreover, these rebellions bore witness to a historical mismatch between ideology and economic structure: they were either ahead of their times (in the modern era) or behind (in the Industrial Age). The mystical religious form of peasant ideology in Müntzer's time was an example of this historical anachronism. We see how this political stance reduces the religious question to a simple expression of a contradiction that is impossible to formulate in appropriate terms. Religious revolutionary speech seems like a phantasmagoric form cut off from real relations, signaling that the time had not yet come for the revolution. Only the contradiction between productive forces and relations of production could lead to a revolutionary overthrow of concrete situations; awareness of these relations is by itself powerless to transform them. The ideology of the peasant wars and Müntzer's eschatological millenarianist proto-communism anticipated the entirely bourgeois consciousness of a time yet to come. Engels's text expresses the conviction that only the working-class proletariat organized in revolutionary class structure could overturn bourgeois society. Its reticence has to do, then, not with peasant traditions but rather with lingering doubts about their capacity to abolish classes. Nevertheless, for Marxists to come, this reading of the first great peasant revolution in the modern era would not resolve their problems in interpretating agrarian struggles.

In contrast to a concept of history where ideas have no power other than heralding a future situation, Ernst Bloch proposed an interpretation of Müntzer's texts where their mystical élan reveals the truth about all revolutionary politics: the necessity of utopia in the radical transformation of an existing order.[14] Bloch set out a philosophy of history where hope, as a form of anticipation for a better future based on the unrealized dreams of the past, is an essential part of the passage toward revolutionary activity. Bloch cited "A Highly Provoked Vindication and a Refutation of the Unspiritual Soft-Living Flesh in Wittenberg" (1524):

> Look, the origin of usury, theft and robbery lies with our lords and princes, who treat all creatures as their possessions: the fish in the water, the birds in the air, the plants on the earth—everything must be theirs, Isaiah 5. And then they proclaim God's commandments to the poor and say: God has commanded that you shall not steal; but that does not help them at all. For while they compel everyone to slave and scrape, the poor peasant, the workman and all who live, Micah 3, if any of the poor commits the smallest crime then he must hang.[15]

For Bloch, religious references and millenarian eschatology were not just the forms of a political discourse that could not be expressed in other terms; they were the very contents of a revolutionary enunciation that had to be mystical in order to be utopian. Therefore, in contrast to Engels, who thought of the proletarian revolution as the norm against which to judge the contents of all insurrectional activities, Bloch thought that the utopian dimension of the peasant war revealed a truth about the possibility of all revolutions.[16] Millenarianism means that the Judgement Day

---

14   Bloch emphasized the messianic dimension of all revolutionary thought. See Ernst Bloch, *Thomas Münzer, théologien de la revolution*, trans. M. de Gandillac (Paris: Les Prairies ordinaires, 2012), 41. [Translator's note: There is no previous English translation of this work. For German, see Bloch, *Thomas Münzer als Theologe der Revolution* (Berlin: Suhrkamp, 1920).]

15   Thomas Müntzer, "Highly Provoked Vindication," trans. Andy Drummond, andydrummond.net.

16   Bloch, *Thomas Münzer*, 87.

will only arrive after a thousand-year reign of justice: the realization of divine justice at the onset of the apocalypse is linked to the idea of earthly justice in the mind of the millenarian thinker. A kingdom of earthly justice must be established in order to see a kingdom of divine justice. For Müntzer and the Anabaptists, as many causes of human suffering were social, Christians could not bear the brunt of suffering that would arrive with the Fall. People cannot suffer properly for theological reasons when already suffering socially. So, in order to suffer theologically on Earth, Christians have to suppress social suffering.

However, there are several important elements missing from Bloch's reading of Müntzer. The theologian's originality consists of linking a certain idea of the apocalypse and the Judgement Day (that is to say, an eschatology, a theory of end-times) to a naturalist vein of thinking against which the appropriation by the feudal lords of all the creatures of the earth can be judged. Müntzer's ideology was characterized by the articulation of three principal philosophies: a denunciation of injustice based on the critique of private property; a religious naturalism that recognized the belonging of all creatures on Earth; and an eschatological mysticism that announced the Apocalypse and Salvation. So, where Engels saw only the expression of class interests (barons against peasants, bourgeois, and plebians) in the ideologies of Luther and Müntzer, Bloch saw also the revolutionary role of religious affects. To understand "the deepest roots of the peasant uprisings," we must go beyond a "purely economic study."[17]

In the specific case of the Peasant War, with its powerful imaginary, and all of its spiritualism, it's impossible—alongside the economic factors that conditioned the unleashing of the conflict and the selection of its objectives—to not consider separately what constitutes their essential and primitive element: the familiarity with the most ancient of dreams, the breakthrough and the expansion of the old heretical movement, the ecstatic will—impatient, rebellious, and serious at its apogee—of a path that leads straight to Paradise. Inclinations, dreams, the most serious and pure emotions, the enthusiasm oriented toward

---

17   Ibid., 87, 88.

end-times that is nourished by a need separate from that which immediately jumps into view and that is never meanwhile a crutch; they
never disappear and their imprint is left for many years to come; they
animate the soul in an original way, bearing the fruit of values; they
survive each empirical catastrophe and bear up wonderfully, prolong-
ing in an unceasing contemporaneity the millenarism that profoundly
shaped the fifteenth century, that of the Peasant War and Anabaptism.[18]

In contrast to Engels, Bloch insisted on the changing rationales of insurrectional activities. So, while Engels presented economic structures that
shape the history of the class struggle, Bloch sought, rather, to identify the
conscious motifs of the passage to praxis. As Bloch writes in one of his
pithy statements, "We don't lay down our lives just to achieve a well-
planned production budget."[19] This points not only to a theoretical—if also
real—opposition between two authors, but to a different perspective:
Engels wanted to understand the property relations that structure class
difference, and Bloch wanted to locate the affective underpinnings of the
revolutionary act. In our time of terrorist messiahs and spiritual ecologies,
Bloch reminds us that a clear awareness of the economic structures of
oppression is rarely by itself enough to constitute a revolutionary *praxis*.

To be sure, the contrast I have struck between the highly materialist
writing of Engels's short text and Bloch's heavily utopian book may seem
a bit like caricature. Yet, the contrast illuminates the wide range of
Marxist positions on the meaning of a peasant movement during the
transition from feudalism to capitalism. For these two authors, the
proto-communist millenarianism of the Anabaptist peasants was a
harbinger; for Engels, it was a sign of its weakness, and for Bloch, it was
a sign of its strength. The uncertainty of whether the peasant wars were
revolutionary or not was due to their taking place at a unique time in
history when people were working to understand what possible alliances
could be formed between worker communism and agrarian socialisms.
As we will see in a moment, Bloch also believed that the revolution must

---

18   Ibid., 89.
19   Ibid., 141.

be placed "under the leadership of the proletariat." Both writers, however, thought that the peasant wars were a "non-contemporaneous contradiction."[20] In order to understand the role that Marxist categories can play in the interpretation of peasant struggles, it is important to situate these categories in places and times where the theory of the proletariat revolution ran up against class-based agrarian societies.

In this context, it bears noting that Latin America has played a central role in the peasant translation of Marxism and the development of indigenous materialism. Having been subjected to European colonialism and American imperialism, South American societies have been sculpted through slavery and the slave trade, the latifundia and plantation system, extractivism and ground rent. These formations have often been geared toward the exportation of raw materials and agricultural products. The integration of an extractivist Latin America into the global market was, moreover, one of the conditions for the emergence of industrial capital. Without gold, silver, and American sugar, the transformation of property relations in Europe would never have developed into global capitalism. In the chapter on primitive accumulation in *Capital*, Marx describes the genesis of the process of the accumulation of capital:

The discovery of gold and silver in America, the extirpation, enslavement, and entombment in mines of the indigenous population of that continent, the beginnings of the conquest and plunder of India, and the conversion of Africa into a preserve for the commercial hunting of blackskins, are all things which characterize the dawn of the era of capitalist production. These idyllic proceedings are the chief moments of primitive accumulation.[21]

We often minimize the colonial dimension of Marx's history of capital. If the "basis of the whole process" is the appropriation of the peasantry in

---

20   Ernst Bloch, *Heritage of Our Times*, trans. Neville Plaice and Stephen Plaice (Cambridge: Polity, 1991), 9.

21   Karl Marx, *Capital: A Critique of Political Economy*, trans. Ben Fowkes (Harmondsworth: Penguin, 1976), 915.

Western Europe, its "snail's pace" would never have accelerated without colonialism's brandishing of the whip.[22] In the colonies, the new capitalist relations of production would never have created a large-scale industrial capitalism. However, Latin America played a special role in this history. As Eduardo Galeano writes,

> Latin America is the region of open veins. Everything, from the discovery until our times, has always been transmuted into European— or later United States—capital, and as such has accumulated in distant centers of power. Everything: the soil, its fruits and its mineral-rich depths, the people and their capacity to work and to consume, natural resources and human resources. Production methods and class structure have been successively determined from outside for each area by meshing it into the universal gearbox of capitalism.[23]

A colonized Latin America has become one of the principal geophysical factories of the West. The extraction of resources necessary for the production of goods is a central link in the world economy. But colonial and postcolonial politics have left the continent underdeveloped.[24] Thrust into the very center of the global market by extractivist practices, postcolonial South American societies have largely been excluded from the progressivist schemes of Western Europe. This must explain a part of the inventiveness of Latin American Marxism. On a continent integrated into the global economy but relegated to the periphery of history by unequal exchanges with Europe, and where the proletariat is almost exclusively peasant and has inherited colonial racial structures, Western Marxist categories have been translated into a language adapted to the peasant and indigenous situation. One of the most fruitful and original of these translations is the work of the Peruvian thinker José Carlos

---

22   Ibid., 876, 914.

23   Eduardo Galeano, *Open Veins of Latin America: Five Centuries of the Pillage of a Continent*, trans. Cedric Belfrage (1973; repr., New York: Monthly Review, 1991), 27.

24   André Gunder Frank, *Latin America: Underdevelopment or Revolution* (New York: Monthly Review, 1969).

Mariátegui. In Mariátegui's South American Marxism, we will witness the return of the *narodniki* sensibility that defined Marx's last years.

The Land Divided: Communism, Peasantry, Indigeneity

Raised by his single mother in a poor family, handicapped by a leg injury, and knowledgeable from a tender age about the rebellions of the lati-fundist laborers he met in the workshop of his grandfather, Mariátegui (1894–1930) became a socially engaged journalist who played a part in the social struggles of his times.[25] He supported the democratic student movements of the Peruvian Republic and was forced to leave the country in 1919. Afterward, he visited Europe, where he met socialist thinkers and organizers. He attended the famous Italian Socialist Party Congress in Livorno in 1921, where the Italian Communist Party was formed. During his European tour, he discovered the thinking of Marx and Georges Sorel. Back in Peru in 1923, he took on the conceptual transla-tion of Marxism in the new context of the struggles for national libera-tion and South American peasant struggles.

While he was a fervent supporter of historical materialism,[26] Mariátegui was also attacked by the Communist International (Comintern) for his "populism" (which is to say his Narodnism), or his unfashionable predilection for forms of Incan communitarian organiza-tion and his refusal to subordinate the questions of the peasantry and indigenous populations to the class struggle led by the industrial prole-tariat.[27] Nicknamed *el amauta*, "the wiseman," in Quechua, he was the main editor of the eponymous magazine *Amauta* founded in 1926,

---

25 See J. Aricó, ed., *Mariátegui y los orígenes del marxismo latino americano* (Mexico: Pasado y Presente, 1978). See also Luis Martínez Andrade, "José Carlos Mariátegui," in J. N. Ducange, R. Keucheyan, and S. Roza, eds., *Histoire globale des socialismes. XIXe–XXIe siècles* (Paris: PUF, 2021).

26 See José Carlos Mariátegui, *Defensa del Marxismo* (Lima: Biblioteca Amauta, 1930). [Translator's note: For a portion of this book in English, see J. C. Mariátegui, "Ethics and Socialism," trans. unknown, *Tricontinental 3* (1967): 20–7.]

27 V. M. Miroshevski, "El 'populismo' en el Peru. Papel de Mariátegui en la histoira del pensamiento social latinoamericano," in Aricó, *Mariátegui y los orígenes*, 57.

which tried to create a synthesis of indigenous anti-imperialism and non-orthodox Marxism.

On the one hand, Mariátegui fought against the American Popular Revolutionary Alliance (APRA) founded by Víctor Raúl Haya de la Torre in 1924, whose anti-imperialist struggle was, for Mariátegui, necessary but limited by the movement's bourgeois flavor. APRA supported the ideological and material independence of Latin America—in particular that of Peru, where it was born—through a joint opposition to American imperialism and Soviet Marxism. Haya de la Torre advocated for Indo-American solutions for the continent, while refusing the vocabulary of the class struggle and Marxist grammar. In short, APRA wanted to establish a politics of liberal reform in order to support the national republic and to develop small individual landholdings. Despite the group's anti-Marxism, Mariátegui found anti-imperialism resources in it that he could use to support a Peruvian path forward toward socialism and hold off the international organs of Bolshevism and their ideology of progress. On the other hand, Mariátegui fought against the Comintern, which had begun to take an interest in Latin America in the 1920s. He founded the Socialist Party of Peru in October 1928, and only in 1930 did he agree to change its name to the Peruvian Communist Party, just before his death at the age of thirty-five, after two years of (often contentious) discussions with the leaders of the Comintern in Latin America. While he had been widely appreciated in the first years of the 1920s for his intellectual rigor and erudition, by the end of the same decade, his interest in nationalism and the peasantry had drawn the scorn of the Comintern.

Mariátegui's Marxism was defined by his desire to return to precolonial Incan settlement practices before they were eradicated by the Conquest of the New World. The commitment to finding a path forward based on the historical existence of an egalitarian agricultural community shaped the contours of a *practical naturalism* where the return to the land was actually a reinvention of communitarian relations, as present before colonization and again after independence. His Marxism was defined by his commitment to the necessity of Marx's translation into the colonial agrarian context. For him, Marxism was not a body of principles with rigid, singular ends under all historical climates and under all social latitudes. Marx drew his method from the intestines of history itself. Marxism, in each country, for every people, operates and acts in its social milieu, and on its environment, without neglecting any of its specificities.[28]

In this speech to the workers' congress in Lima, he announced the themes that he would take up again in *Defensa del marxismo*. Unfortunately, his project of forging an alliance between the peasantry and the proletariat in a socialist political party that paid attention to the rights of the indigenous peoples and valued agrarian relations led to his being accused of "racism" and "populism" by the Comintern.[29]

In 1941, the Soviet academic Miroshevski launched a critique of populism, and this critique led to a controversy between the two about the founding of the Communist Party in Peru. Mariátegui refused to transform a socialist party that had been dedicated to laborers and peasants into the Communist Party modeled on the Comintern's mandates, because he did not want to subordinate the peasant fight for ownership of the land—and indigenous struggles for racial equality that came with it—to the industrial proletariat's struggle. This strategic divergence expressed a philosophical difference in their conceptions of history: different from the thinking of the Comintern, Mariátegui believed that the paths toward communisms were as many and as particular as the historical conditions in the world. He saw for Peru a specific path forward, anchored in the class structure and in the "racial" structure of the young independent republic. In a country where four-fifths of the proletariat were indigenous peasants, the socialist solution could only be

---

28   José Carlos Mariátegui, "Mensaje al congreso obrero (1927)," in *Ideología y política* (Lima: Amauta, 1971), 112.

29   Robert Paris, preface to José Carlos Mariátegui, *Sept essais d'interprétation de la réalité péruvienne*, trans. R. Mignot (Paris: Maspero, 1968), 56. It is worth noting that the accusation of racism had a very different sense (in fact opposite) from how it is used today: for the Comintern, racism was the explication of social phenomena from the standpoint of racial concepts and not from the basis of class struggle.

based on agrarian reform and an alliance of indigenous peasants and urban laborers. Many scholars have tried to rehabilitate Mariátegui from "baseless" accusations of populism and indigenism. José Aricó, who stands at the forefront of these scholars, casts doubt on the populist "foundation" of his work, an interpretation that is based on a "lack of knowledge" about his work:

> These criticisms are directed toward his supposed "populism" and a whole slew of offshoots developed from there: his liberal opinions about the indigenous problem, which he refused to accept was a "national problem," his concessions to the dictates of APRA, his resistance to the formation of a proletarian party, etc.[30]

Aricó believed that these defamatory accusations had a political goal: they wanted to undercut his efforts to create a specific path of development toward Latin American communism, which would not bypass capitalism but would permit the emancipation of the indigenous peasants based upon a "return" to the rural commune. In the context of the Third International and the struggle against the Socialist Revolutionaries in Russia, these ends were quickly rejected. While these accusations meant to discredit him, it's nevertheless not entirely clear that Mariátegui was so far removed from the populist ideals as his defenders make him out to be.

Rather, Mariátegui's concern for forms of precapitalist life and his desire to give back to the rural Andean masses the power that they had had in the Incan system led him back to a *sensibility of ecological Narodnism* immanent in historical materialism, if it was never its greatest part. Michael Löwy writes on this theme:

> Called "petit bourgeois socialism" by its critics, this position is nothing other than the one suggested by Marx in his letter to Zasulich (a letter unknown to Mariátegui). In both, we find the deep insight that modern socialism, especially in countries with an agrarian structure,

---

30   Aricó, *Mariátegui y los orígenes*, xxxv, xl.

will have to *dig into* the vernacular traditions, into the collective memory of the peasants and the masses, into the social and cultural remnants of a precapitalist and communitarian way of life, into the practices of cooperation, solidarity, and collective property of the rural *Gemeinschaft*.[31]

Löwy is right to insist on the extensive similarities between Russian populism and Peruvian indigenism. In both, a multilinear philosophy of history emphasized the concrete circumstances of each social formation, insomuch as each was the contingent result of the hybridization of the old and the new. Temporality was no longer linear or oriented toward progress, insomuch as the desired future, the *eschaton*, is the "heroic" return to the past rather than a telos, or a necessary advent of the new.[32] The modern forgoes the compulsion for progress in order to be realized in the remnants of tradition. This tradition would be based on collective property relations through which practices of solidarity and cooperation would develop. This vision of a community, or of a rural Gemeinschaft, breathes new life into a social ideal that not only concerns economic or politic institutions but also nature itself in its interpersonal relations, and in their affective density in the absence of a state-based rationalization of social relations.[33] The rural Gemeinschaft would demonstrate the relations and practices of collective property relations that form the basis of the community and the utopian norm of a desirable future. In Mariátegui, the issue was not exactly a "return to the land"; instead, it was a return to the community where the wealth of interpersonal relations comes from collective property. The land community was the basis for social relations that were less alienated.

---

31   Michael Löwy, "L'indigénisme marxiste de José Carlos Mariátegui," *Actuel Marx* 56 (2014): 13–22.

32   José Carlos Mariátegui, "Aniversario y Balance (1928)," in *Ideología y política*, 112.

33   Löwy took the term "Gemeinschaft," of which he is quite fond, from the sociologist Ferdinand Tönnies. See Ferdinand Tönnies, *Community and Society* (1887), trans. Charles P. Loomis (London: Routledge, 1999); Michael Löwy, *The War of Gods: Religion and Politics in Latin America* (London: Verso, 1996), 60.

That Mariátegui was ignorant of Marx's discussions with populists would seem to be confirmed by commentators.[34] Yet, he was up to date, for the most part, with the situation of the Russian commune, as the following passage from *Seven Interpretive Essays on Peruvian Reality* makes clear, where he established a parallel between the *mir* and the *ayllu*, the Andean agricultural commune:

> Feudalism similarly let rural communes continue in Russia, a country that offers an interesting parallel because in its historical process it is much closer to these agricultural and semifeudal countries than are the capitalist countries of the West . . . Under the system of landlords, the Russian mir, like the Peruvian community, was completely denaturalized.[35]

In *Seven Interpretive Essays*, Mariátegui's most important work, he translates the categories of political economy to the peasant, indigenous context of Peru. In each essay, he shows how the questions that socialists pose usually in cultural terms as the "education of the masses" were actually based on property relations, which determine the appropriation of nature, the organization of labor, and the division of social wealth. The political problem of the place of Indians in postcolonial Peruvian society was not a cultural problem of under-education (of the oppressed or the oppressors) but an economic problem of the separation from property of the means of agrarian production, beginning with the most important of these means: the land.

In the passage above, Mariátegui is not interested merely in establishing a metaphorical relation between the forms of the organization of production in the *mir* and the *ayllu*. Instead, he constructs an analogy between these two communal forms and the type of disturbance that they suffered due to feudalism (in the Russian case) and colonization (in the Peruvian case). This correspondence allows us to establish a

---

34   See, in particular, Aricó, *Mariátegui y los orígenes*.
35   José Carlos Mariátegui, *Seven Interpretive Essays on Peruvian Reality*, trans. Marjory Urquidi (Austin: University of Texas Press, 1971), 58–9.

historical mechanism: the development of feudalism or colonialism leads to a qualitative modification in the agricultural commune, without its wholesale destruction. The characteristic phenomenon in this evolution is the reduction of communal lands to the point that they no longer meet the needs of the peasants. Their dependence on plantation owners, colonizers, or the market only grows. The analogy with the Russian case allows us to describe a transition toward forms of non-capitalist private appropriation. The transition toward feudalism in Russia or toward colonialism in Peru nevertheless allowed cooperative methodologies to persist within rural communes. For Mariátegui, it was not necessary that a capitalist period intervene before the development of large-scale cooperation. To the contrary: the persistence of agrarian collectivism in the communes allows us to imagine a communist future that traces out the historical experience of capitalism. The liberal measures of the republic did not allow for any confrontation with the land-owning class of colonial plantations; rather, it brought about the development of small, individual landholdings where a communal organization of production reigned in the *ayllus*:

> If the latter had been dissolved and expropriated by a capitalism in vigorous and independent growth, it would have been considered a casualty of economic progress. The Indian would have passed from a mixed system of communism and servitude to a system of free wages. Although this change would have denaturalized him somewhat, it would have placed him in a position to organize and emancipate himself as a class, like the other proletariats of the world. However, the gradual expropriation and absorption of the "community" by the latifundium not only plunged him deeper into servitude, but also destroyed the economic and legal institution that helped safeguard the spirit and substance of his ancient civilization.[36]

At the end of this period, some of the peasantry fulfilled the role of statute labor on the big plantations, and some was free in the rural

---

36 Ibid., 67.

communes, the *ayllus*, which still upheld communal property laws. Some peasants were part of both systems, since they lived in the communes: circumstances that guaranteed their means of subsistence but obligated them to perform statute labor on the plantations. After independence in Peru, state laws curtailed the power of the *ayllus* while never addressing that of the plantations. The commune lost its autonomy and was swallowed up by the large latifundist properties. Consequently, liberal reforms of land ownership never developed a free peasant proletariat capable of organizing itself into a revolutionary class as in Western countries. Without being a free class of laborers, that is to say, capable of selling their labor power for a wage, the postcolonial peasantry could not self-organize according to the same modalities as the Western urban proletariat. The colonial history of plantations and liberal agrarian reforms led to the development of a hybrid society. Though the aim was to limit the power of the plantations while developing small individual landholdings, in keeping with the rosy ideal of bourgeois equality, what ended up happening was the dismantling of the agrarian communes to the benefit of the plantation owners. The collectivist history represented by these communes grew increasingly distant as their hold on territory waned. Capitalist relations of production had not yet developed, but "primitive communism" was dead in the water. What was born was a feudal and colonial society with republican institutions, integrated in the global capitalist market. From that point forward, it would be self-evident that the similarities between Mariátegui's thinking and the *narodniki* were neither random nor superficial. Mariátegui's motifs were the three essential positions of Russian populism.

First, the autonomous development of socialism in Peru presupposed the existence of a multiplicity of temporalities and historical trajectories worldwide. In "Anniversario y balance" (Anniversary and stocktaking), Mariátegui wrote with the independent-minded spirit that is found in the Russian populists:

> Of course, we don't want Latin American socialism to be a calque or a copy. It must be a heroic creation. By the reality that is ours, by our

own language, we must give life to Indo-American socialism. This is a mission worthy of the new generation.[37]

Second, on the issue the land itself, Mariátegui discovered communitarian property relations in the Russian commune that were similar to those on the *ayllu*. Finally, from a strategic point of view, the fact that the archaic commune was the utopian norm of revolutionary action implied that the development of socialism could never be constrained by a single political and historical direction. In sum, there is enough evidence to confirm Mariátegui's populism without caving in to knee-jerk critiques of it. As Miroshevski wrote in 1941:

> Writing about the character of the autochthonous community, Mariátegui concluded that there was a "natural tendency for the indigenous to subscribe to communism." This conclusion reminds us in a rather striking fashion of the opinions of Russian "populists" on the "collectivist spirit of the Russian peasantry."[38]

The collectivist spirit of the Andean peasants would be founded on the inherited social practices of the agricultural commune that the Incan Empire "captured" without corrupting. This detour into "Incan communism" implied a return to collectivist relations with the land thanks to which a socialist future was possible.

"Incan Communism" and the Revolutionary Myth

The notion of Incan Communism is definitely one of the most disputed of Mariátegui's ideas. Taking up the work of the Peruvian sociologist Hildebrando Castro Pozo (1890–1945) on the *ayllu* and the development of agrarian collectivism in the Andes, Mariátegui argued that the

---

37 Mariátegui, "Aniversario y Balance," 249.
38 V. M. Miroshevski, "El 'populismo' en el Peru," in Aricó, *Mariátegui y los orígenes*, 68.

Incan Empire was able to develop due to the model of the Andean agricultural commune and collective land ownership.[39] Whether Pozo and Mariátegui were beholden to a profoundly ahistorical or empirically false position, or whether they emphasized the critical and strategic function of this usage of Peruvian history, all commentators agree about the anachronistic bent of this thinking.[40] Yet, there are few who have bothered to make the distinction that Mariátegui commonly made between archaic and modern forms of communism, which allowed him to think more about the mythical status of revolutionary strategies.

In the Incan Empire before the Conquest of the New World, imperial institutions were based on the raising of a tribute tax and statute labor. These institutions emerged from a dense network of *ayllus*, a social structure formed of several families but that tended to lose its familial character to take on an increasingly territorial dimension. As Sergio de Santis has noted, this regime of landed property evolved from a largely collectivist model—cooperative labor on communal lands and individual labor on lands granted to each family—to a tripartite model where the peasant masses tilled Incan lands (centralized power), the lands of the sun (religious power), and communal lands in rotation. According to de Santis, the division of lands—defined by the rotation of lands among families—and communal exploitation were maintained throughout the empire during the colonial period.[41] The argument for the metaphorical existence of an "indigenous communism," in other words a "tradition" or "communist spirit" among the Andean peasantry, can be understood in the context of the absence of private property and the existence of collective labor practices.[42] Yet, Mariátegui's argument was much more

---

39   Castro Pozo Hildebrando, *Del ayllu al cooperativismo socialista* (Lima: Jiron Puno, 1936).

40   See Michael Löwy, "Communism and Religion: José Carlos Mariátegui's Revolutionary Mysticism," trans. M. O. Breña, *Latin American Perspective* 35, no. 2 (March 2008): 71–9; and Donald V. Kingsbury, "Book Review: *José Carlos Mariátegui: An Anthology*," *Historical Materialism* 4, no. 21 (2013): 257–72.

41   Sergio de Santis, "Les communautés de village chez les Incas, les Aztèques et les Mayas. Contribution à l'étude du mode de production asiatique," *La Pensée* 122 (August 1965): 88.

42   Mariátegui, *Seven Interpretive Essays*, 71, 68.

audacious: he believed that the tributary, hierarchical, and authoritarian system of the Incas was an anticipatory form of communism. "Here we find an institution that survives from the autochthonous regime, an institution that categorically demonstrates that the Inca organization was a communist organization," he wrote.[43] So, regardless of the disputable empirical reality of the communist character of Incan life (founded on the extraction of surplus labor by taxation), he argues for the cultural and historical relativism of communism:

> Modern communism is different from Inca communism. This is the first thing that must be learned and understood by the scholar who delves into Tawantinsuyo. The two communisms are products of different human experiences. They belong to different historical epochs. They were evolved by dissimilar civilizations. The Inca civilization was agrarian; the civilization of Marx and Sorel is industrial. In the former, man submitted to nature; in the latter, nature sometimes submits to man. It is therefore absurd to compare the forms and institutions of the two communisms. All that can be compared is their essential and material likeness, within the essential and material difference of time and space. And this comparison requires a certain degree of historical relativism.[44]

Three core tenets of Mariátegui's thought are apparent here. First, there is no one single model of communism with universal institutions and rules. The word itself marks only a form of organization of social relations founded on the absence of private property, a form that can be modified according to the multiplicity of distinct political regimes. Communism appears as a utopian ideal, to the extent that its invariant principle must always be brought up to date and particularized in political organizations adapted to the social formation in question. The Peruvian thinker refused the idea of a "model" communism, which would be an ethnocentric representation of history where "belated"

---

43   Ibid., 228.
44   Ibid., 81.

social formations must follow the path of "advanced" formations. Second, Mariátegui did not remove "the cumbersome despotic aspects of the system in order to exalt pure 'communism.'"[45] Instead, careful about historical differences, he distinguished Incan communism founded on the absence of individual freedom from "the complex liberal philosophy" born of modernity.[46] He added,

> To believe that the abstract idea of liberty is of the same substance as the concrete image of a liberty with a Phrygian cap—daughter of Protestantism and the French Revolution—is to be trapped by an illusion that may be due to a mere, but not disinterested, philosophical astigmatism of the bourgeoisie and of democracy.[47]

For Mariátegui, communism could, under certain circumstances, be theocratic and despotic. It did not guarantee the absence of religious belief or individual freedoms. While this might sound like the justification for the imposition of an authoritarian system, it must, to the contrary, be understood as a critique of Stalinist authoritarianism: while there is in each era a certain dominant idea of communism, communism cannot develop in the modern, liberal era without respecting the rights of citizens. Mariátegui writes, "Although autocracy and communism are now incompatible, they were not so in primitive societies."

Third, the difference between modern and Incan communism is based on a distinction between an agrarian civilization where "in the former, man submitted to nature and in the latter nature sometimes submits to man." These are ways of relating to nature that mark different eras of communism. We find a typology of political systems while studying the environmental history of societies. European modernity is "atheist," liberal, and based on dominating the land, whereas agrarian civilization recognized in practice the belonging of people to the land. Ways of relating to the land are, then, a definitive particularization of the communist

---

45   Santis, "Les communautés," 88.
46   Mariátegui, *Seven Interpretive Essays*, 82.
47   Ibid., 82.

idea. More precisely stated, the *ayllu*, in the understanding of Castro Pozo and Mariátegui, is "the realization of a 'perfect correlation' between humans and nature," where the Indian community is still a living organism.[48] Certain property relations would guarantee richer interpersonal relations that were also more varied and more dense, to the extent that the uses of the land that they authorized did not arise from a logic of subjugating nature. Mariátegui cited one of the primary works of Andean indigenism, *From the Ayllu to the Empire* by Luis E. Valcárcel (1891–1987):

> Valcárcel, in his study of the economic life of Tawantinsuyo, writes that "the land, in native tradition, is the common mother; from her womb come not only food but man himself. Land provides all wealth. The cult of Mama Pacha is on a par with the worship of the sun and, like the sun, Mother Earth represents no one in particular. Joined in the aboriginal ideology, these two concepts gave birth to agrarianism, which combines communal ownership of land and the universal religion of the sun."[49]

This Quechua concept bears witness to the fact that indigenism—as a political movement aiming to counteract the forms of racism and oppression specific to Indians—was, from the beginning, a form of "agrarianism," that is to say, that it developed from an Indian mythology associated with European cultural forms founded on an economic problem of the division of the land. More precisely stated, the evocation of a communitarian past aimed to guarantee a juridical and political equality between racialized groups suffering under dominant social systems (Indian, Creole, Black). This egalitarianism was legitimized by indigenous naturalism formulated in a symbolic modern system (universal religion). Agrarianism and indigenism were not "authentic" cosmologies of homogeneous and ahistorical social groups. They were, rather,

---

48   Robert Paris, "José Carlos Mariátegui et le modèle du 'communism' inca," *Annales Économies, Sociétés, Civilisations* 21, no. 5 (1966): 1071; Mariátegui, *Seven Interpretive Essays*, 68.

49   Ibid., 52–3.

ontological hybridizations of autochthonous thinking and European categories in a postcolonial social context where these societies were forced to confront the economic problem of the division of the land. Indigenism and agrarianism were strategic reactions to European capital's domination of nature and non-white people. The "universal religion" of Indians (the worship of Pachamama) can, then, be understood as the "translation" of a non-modern, Quechua cosmology into a typically modern sign system, that is, the *natural religion* of European revolutionary philosophers. The anti-modern function of the naturalist indigenous myth (of egalitarian communitarian relations based on the belonging of all life to a common Earth, in the face of colonialism and capitalism) is evident in one of the most typical forms of modernity, namely, natural rights (universal nature serving as the juridical norm in the framework of rational religion). The material relation of the ancient Incans to the land is the mythological foundation of Mariátegui "Incan" communism that revived communism through indigenous cosmologies. Incan communism was as much a utopia as a historical reality.

Donald Kingsbury goes so far as to say that Incan communism was what Mariátegui called all indigenous forms of resistance against capitalist modernization as long as they were both oppositional and supported "agrarian communism."[50] For Mariátegui, it wasn't that cultural difference needed to be the basis of resistance to progress; rather, he wanted to show how the belief in an ideal society infused with myth and religion could allow a practical critique of modernity: "For Mariátegui, socialism was inseparable from an attempt to re-enchant the world."[51] The theory of Incan communism must be thought of from the standpoint of Mariátegui's thinking on the role of myth in historical materialism.

Incan communism represents the historical counterpoint to capitalist property relations and a critique of "disenchanted" modern rationality, as Max Weber would say.[52] The form of rationality that is thought to

---

50   Kingsbury, "Book Review," 264.
51   Ibid., 271.
52   Max Weber, *Complete Writings on Academic and Political Vocations*, ed. J. Dreijmanis, trans. G. C. Wells (New York: Algora, 2008), 44.

demystify the world is, for Mariátegui, one of the central problems of historical materialism because it preempts and excludes all other forms of rationality. On one hand, the secularization of thought devalorizes a host of practices and indigenous representations that are then reabsorbed back into the realm of tradition or, in the worst-case scenario, revalorized as superstition. In the first case, these are inherited behaviors which are not based on rational parameters but that always and forever await rationalization; in the second case, they are errors, or beliefs that can only be acknowledged in the course of being abandoned or cast aside. In both cases, myths are criticized from the standpoint of modern rationality and the more "advanced" character of modern social formations. On the other hand, the absence of myth leads neither to thought nor action, and this has a political dimension that must be considered.[53] Mariátegui contends that "neither rationality nor science can become myths."[54] Myths are important for him because they have an affective dimension capable of unsettling consciousness and spurring action. Rather than the structure of their etiologies, what now distinguishes myth from rationality is efficaciousness in mobilizing action. In terms of energy and quantitative measure, myths are seen as vectors of an affective flux capable of inciting action, whereas rationality is noted most for its ontological inefficacy.

From this perspective, modern religion is only the institution that has taken charge of the affective power of ancient myths. Criticism of religion is therefore not only lodged in vain but, moreover, is a "liberal bourgeois pastime" to the extent that it lacks social life's utopian and affective contents.[55] Inversely, historical materialism, as a theory of revolutionary practice, is for Mariátegui "a religious, mystical, spiritual force."[56] As has been noted since the 1980s by the "theologians of liberation" in Latin

---

53 Mariátegui, *Seven Interpretive Essays*, 136.

54 H. E. Vanden and M. Becker, eds., *José Carlos Mariátegui: An Anthology* (New York: Monthly Review, 2011), 383.

55 Mariátegui, *Seven Interpretive Essays*, 136.

56 José Carlos Mariátegui, "El hombre y el mito," *El Mundial*, January 16, 1925, in Luis Martínez Andrade, *Écologie et Libération. Critique de la modernité dans la théologie de la libération* (Paris: Van Dieren, 2016), 9.

America, his philosophy of history can only be understood from the perspective of the Christian mythology that it wants to reanimate.[57]

Gustavo Gutiérrez Merino believes that Mariátegui's work is based on a political eschatology inherited from Christianity whose philosophy of history has been laid out and thematized by Ernst Bloch. Gutiérrez Merino lays out how Bloch's "philosophy of hope" clarifies three basic dimensions of Mariátegui's thinking: first, myth, as the affective power of mobilization and action, plays the same role that hope does for Bloch. It's a psychic representation of "what is not yet" because it is still "not yet conscious."[58] Second, the advent of what has not yet taken shape presupposes an awareness of what could have happened in the past and what, in a utopian projection, can take place in the future. Third, this utopian relation to the past takes the form, for Bloch and Mariátegui, of a "deeply rooted" relation to the land. The revolutionary power of that which has not yet taken shape, the representation of an eschatological time in the form of a projection of the utopian past, and the return to the land as a reconciliation of contrary impulses of capitalism are the three aspects of Mariátegui's thinking that the philosophy of hope can help clarify.

In the 1920s and 1930s, the presence of various indigenous struggles for power in Latin American and the rise of fascism in Germany posed problems that have a similar aspect: Is it possible to have a revolutionary concept of history without inventing a utopian past defined by rooting in the land and a belonging to the earth? The problem raised at the beginning of this chapter returns: Is every agrarian interpretation of communism necessarily linked to a utopian representation of an original unity of societies and nature?

---

57 Liberation theology is a part of the Roman Catholic Church, begun in the late 1970s by bishops and clergy inspired by Franciscan and Jesuit struggles against the Conquest of the New World as well as by the theory of dependence and by Marxism. See Gustavo Gutiérrez Merino, *A Theology of Liberation: History, Politics and Salvation*, trans. Sister Caridad Inda and John Eagleson (New York: Orbis, 1988). For a classical commentary on liberation theology, please see Löwy, *The War of Gods*, and Martínez Andrade, *Écologie et Libération*.

58 Gutiérrez Merino, *A Theology of Liberation*, 123.

The Land: A Non-contemporaneous Contradiction

Our current detour through Leipzig is not based on real conversations between Bloch and Mariátegui, an explicit filiation between their thinking, or known intertextuality. Rather, it is almost certain they never knew of one another and never read each other's work. Mariátegui spent most of his life in Lima, even if he did travel to Europe, and Bloch spent his life in Leipzig, even if he lived in the US during World War II. My comparison of their work is justified by the theological and decolonial readings of this chapter. At the same time, the work of both thinkers bears witness to a non-progressive view of history that is attentive to the power of myths in political practice and sensitive to the problem of the "roots" of the peasantry. More precisely stated, Bloch's philosophy allows us to think about the revolutionary role of "belonging" to the earth at the same time as it presents the risks of a philosophy of rootedness.

Before his magisterial trilogy *The Principle of Hope*,[59] it was *Heritage of Our Times*, published in 1935, where the "Marxist Schelling" took up the problem of the relation to the land as a utopian principle.[60] For Bloch, utopia is the projection into the future of the past's unrealized desires for emancipation, which inspire the revolutionary transformation of the present. In *Heritage of Our Times*, he searched to understand Nazism, the reasons for its success, and the causes of the communist movement's failures in Germany. German fascism scored a notable triumph in being able to tap into the utopian aspirations of *what has not yet come to mind*,[61] which the worker movement had never mobilized. Nazism mixed a "fanatical religious bond with the soil" with the

---

59   This is Bloch's seminal work, which appeared in East Germany between 1954 and 1959. It marks the final rupture with Stalinian systems. See Ernst Bloch, *The Principle of Hope*, trans. Neville Plaice, Stephen Plaice, and Paul Knight (Oxford: Basil Blackwell, 1986).

60   Jürgen Habermas, "Ein marxistischer Schelling. Zu Ernst Blochs spekulativem Materialismus," in *Theorie und Praxis. Sozialphilosophische Studien*, vol. 2 (Frankfurt: Suhrkamp, 1971).

61   Bloch's expression is "Noch-Nicht-Bewusste." See Bloch, *The Principle of Hope*, 117.

heretical Christian socialist millenarianism (the third reign of Joachim de Flore).[62] However, this "bond" was not necessarily the sign of a naive "archaism" or a reactionary tendency: rather, it bore witness to an unresolved contradiction in the past, which holds within it a messianic urge for the transformation of the present:

> Home, soil, and nation are such *objectively* raised contradictions of the traditional to the capitalist Now, in which they have been increasingly destroyed and not replaced. They are contradictions of the traditional to the capitalist Now and elements of ancient society which have not yet died: they were contradictions even in their origin, namely to the past forms which never in fact wholly realized the intended contents of home, soil, and nation.[63]

Facing the banality of capitalism's destructiveness of traditional social formations, Bloch's originality is that he maintains the permanence of cultural forms or, at a minimum, the remnants of the unsatisfied desires that they had once spurred. The contradiction between the "traditional" and the "capitalist now" is only the contemporary repetition of a past contradiction (and it's surely the repetitive character of history that explains, through a mise-en-abîme, the repetition of set phrases in Bloch's words above). This contradiction is between the destructive logic of capitalism and the "wishful images," or the unrealized desires contained within the terms "home, soil, nation."[64] The progressive disappearance of forms of life linked to communitarian and traditional organizations did not destroy the dreams to which they gave birth. No one can deny the destiny of the concepts of *Heimat*, *Boden*, or *Volk* when Bloch wrote these lines in 1935 in Germany. As paradoxical as the weight of their utopian sentiment may be, it relied upon a distinction between a "contemporary contradiction" and a "noncontemporaneous contradiction," which allowed the establishment of a worker-based political

---

62   Bloch, *Heritage of Our Times*, 140.
63   Ibid., 109.
64   Ibid., 78.

strategy capable of taking into account the racism and anti-Semitism of class-based societies.[65]

Bloch differentiated between two types of contradictions: contemporaneous and noncontemporaneous. Each can be subjective—and so pertaining to representations of the mind; or objective—which is to say, anchored in the very structure of social relations. The contradictions rampant in "home, soil, nation" are not just subjective; they rely on *what has not yet come to mind*, where past antagonisms have not yet been *objectively* realized. Since the beginning of the sixteenth century, peasant wars have carried forward the millenarian dreams that set real misery against the hope of a kingdom of God on Earth. While the objective contradictions that produced them have disappeared (the exploitation of a servile peasantry by feudal lords), their dreams of equality and justice are still alive, if as political platforms of reactionary ideologues rather than in a communist movement. *Home, soil,* and *nation* bear witness to a desire for "rootedness" that the liberal bourgeoisie generally scorned and that communism seemed incapable of bringing about, and yet that reactionary politics has revived.[66] There are two problems, however. First, why did Bloch not see this opposition as a "genuinely contemporaneous contradiction"? And, secondly, what political effects arise from this form of non-contemporaneity?

In Bloch's thinking, the "genuinely contemporaneous contradiction" is based on the antagonism between capital and labor, which is the basic social relation of our times.[67] What belongs to our times is the "genuinely contemporary," or the new, as opposed to the inherited, or the old. But whereas the contradictions of the present must find their future resolution, "authentic contemporaneity" is objectively that which brings about a future that has not yet arrived, just as non-contemporaneity is the trace of a past contradiction that has not yet been resolved. "The heritage of

---

65 See the famous chapter "Summary Transition: Non-contemporaneity and Obligation to Its Dialectic," in ibid., 97–148.

66 Ibid., 50–1.

67 Ibid., 113.

our times" is, then, what we have inherited from the past (genuinely
noncontemporaneous contradictions) and what we leave in place for the
future (genuinely contemporaneous contradictions that will become
genuinely non-contemporaneous). In Bloch's work, the contemporaneous and the noncontemporaneous indicate historical contradictions,
which is to say, relations between antagonistic groups and incompatible
phenomena that exist only through their opposition with an adversarial
group or contrary phenomenon, respectively. It is only contradictions
that are contemporaneous or noncontemporaneous, because only they
are invested with historicity, that is to say, a becoming inherent within
relation itself. The opposition between two realities that exist only relative to each other but that never can be realized fully in this relation leads
to a movement of transformation inherent in relation itself. The contradiction is the expression of the antagonism of class relations, past or
present. Why, then, is the attachment to the land specifically a noncontemporaneous contradiction?

First, it bears witness to the peasantry's "doggedness in being rooted
which comes from the matter they cultivate, which directly sustains and
feeds them; they are fixed in the ancient soil and in the cycle of the
seasons."[68] The first reason of this attachment to the land is material: the
practices of reproduction and the routines to which these practices give
rise. The culture of the land produces a social historicity founded on
cycles and repetition, which reproduces the cycles of nature. The timing
of the modes of agrarian production is dependent on the timing of the
seasons; the temporal structure is inseparable from meteorological vari-
ance and the knowledge of time's passage, which is dependent on the
weather. Second, the peasant "is harder to displace by the machine than
the craftsman a hundred years ago."[69] Belonging to a rural community,
which is in part defined by kinship, guarantees landownership. This
tendency to transmit the peasant's patrimony assures the reproduction
of inherited property relations and closes a resistance to the capitalist
transformation of the countryside. We can note as well the resemblance

---

68   Ibid., 100.
69   Ibid., 99.

in this thinking to Max Weber's "Capitalism and Rural Society," in which Weber insists on the difference between the US situation, where the rural community never existed, and the German case, where the community, which was based on specific property relations and on a particular form of sociability, slowed capitalist development in the countryside.[70] Different from Weber, however, Bloch sees in rural life a potentially radical force ready to oppose capitalism. Instead of seeing in the rural community merely the tendency to resistance, Bloch sees in it a revolutionary potential, whether communist or fascist.

Finally, the third reason for rootedness is comparable to "the attachment of the primitive man to the soil which contains the spirits of his ancestors."[71] To the degree that the soil is the objective condition of the reproduction of life, and to the extent that the relation to the land is assured by property relations that guarantee patrimony's succession, the soil is both the catalyst of future reproduction and the guarantor of the heritage of the past. The land guarantees the community's historical continuity, and this history can take the shape of mysticism or religion, or an animism whose legitimacy Bloch never doubts. The soil is the material basis for practices that capitalism's logic aims to destroy. The land is living because it belonged to ancestors who, having lived there, transmitted it as a basis of the life of individuals and as a material basis for the reproduction of the group. Belonging to the group is mediated by the ownership of land which is transmitted through the community. Thus, it seems clear that the relation of belonging to the land, as a subjective dimension of an objective contradiction (the opposition of the peasantry to all forms of the expropriation that it had known in history), is not genuinely

---

70   We know that Bloch was very close to Weber, and that Bloch was a member of the student group that worked with the sociologist every Sunday afternoon, which served as the occasion for his first meeting with Lukács. There is a subtextual conversation about this in "Capitalism and Rural Society." There, Weber argued on behalf of the rural communities that were disappearing due to the destruction of "semi-communist" systems and the end of slavery. See Peter Ghosh, ed., "Max Weber on 'The Rural Community': A Critical Edition of the English Text," *History of European Ideas* 31, no. 3 (2005): 327–66.

71   Bloch, *Heritage of Our Times*, 102.

contemporaneous for Bloch, just as is the conflict between the proletariat and the bourgeoisie.

Fascism marks the success of capital in maintaining control over the
proletariat to the degree that it has assimilated the mysticism of the land
into its program for "self-integration into the ancestral peasant blood
kinship."[72] This is what explains its "success." It is also important to note
that the fact of the noncontemporaneity of claims to the land and belonging are not "over," but that they express instead the "*incomplete* wealth of
the past."[73] This allows us to understand what the noncontemporaneity
of the attachment to the land implies in terms of a political strategy.

Rootedness: A Noncontemporaneous Politics

Bloch's interpretation of fascism as a non-contemporaneous politics has
two major political implications. First, a refusal to believe in the ideology
of progress has, as a corollary, the idea of a future that is invented through
a heroism that unseats present and past contradictions. The ancient
cannot be considered over and done with, and the past cannot be thought
of as archaic. Revolutionary power comes from the capacity of "anticipatory consciousness" to predict the resolution of contradictions not yet
perceived in the present by their projection into an eschatology of the
end of times.[74] But this philosophy of history also finds in the past the
sources for hope (in a subjective belief in the revolutionary possibility)
and the residual contradictions that action can resolve (in an objective
contradiction of a non-resolved past). Still more radically, Bloch believed
that the noncontemporary contradictions the present has inherited from
the past—the attachment to the land, for example—are constitutive from
the beginning of the "subjectively contemporaneous contradiction": "the
free revolutionary action of the proletariat."[75] So, in what sense can we

---

72   Ibid., 140.
73   Ibid., 116.
74   See the second part of Bloch's *The Principle of Hope*.
75   Bloch, *Heritage of Our Times*, 113.

say that the desire for rootedness is linked to a communist politics? We find an answer to this question in the following passage:

> The factors of non-contemporaneous contradiction which are—as we have shown—powerless for sudden change have thus nevertheless, sentimentally or romantically, already recalled that wholeness and liveliness from which Communism draws genuine matter against alienation, from which, alongside Communism, degeneration, attachment to space, and arcadian-Dionysian "nature" are confusedly rampant again today. As creation which was not satisfied, as portent and witness to spheres which at least make the *problem* of a multi-layered wholeness the duty of the dialectic which is merely associated with capitalism in an all too single-layered way.[76]

In Bloch's philosophy, attachment to the land and rootedness in the land are "moments of noncontemporaneous contradiction"; they are desires emerging from the "hunger" for freedom—this universal historical experience in the conditions of alienation. "Sentimental" or "Romantic" elements are particular cultural forms in which unrealized desires of preceding historical situations arise. The contemporaneous subjective contradiction is not by itself enough; it is a "too single-layered" dialectic that does not provide enough of the elements of the "anticipatory consciousness" for it to be truly revolutionary.[77] For this reason alone, certain noncontemporaneous contradictions were adopted from the beginning by the revolutionary movement: for example, "Rousseau's arcadian 'nature'" which bore witness to a "hidden universalism" is the subversive element from out of which utopia can be conceived.[78] In other words, positive, utopian contents must be given to the revolution for its critical and destructive dimension to be effective. The noncontemporaneous contradictions that were never previously resolved, like the myth of attachment to the land, form the basis of the revolutionary imagination. While the subjectively contemporaneous

---

76 Ibid., 112.
77 Bloch, *The Principle of Hope*, vol. 1, 195.
78 Bloch, *Heritage of Our Times*, 112.

contradiction (the free will of the proletariat) does not lead to the recuperation of the hopes of the subjectively noncontemporaneous contradictions (homeland, soil, people), it abandons the fury of "degeneration, attachment to space, and arcadian-Dionysian 'nature'" to the power of reactionary politics. The contemporaneity of noncontemporaneous contradictions (whose contents are set by homeland, soil, and people) pose the ontological problem of the definition of totality: how can different "layers" of social reality exist at once in the same totality? Bloch proposes a definition of social totality:

> A multi-temporal and multi-spatial dialectic, the polyrhythmics and the counterpoint of such a dialectic are thus precisely the instrument of the *mastered* final stage or totality; naturally not of absolutely every one, but of the critical, the non-contemplative, the practically intervening one.[79]

No single contradiction can summarize a historical era in its entirety. Capitalism itself, as a "dominated" stage of a theoretical totality, that is to say, as the moment where non-capitalist differences are wiped out by the conflict between labor and capital, cannot bring together all the contradictions of the time under its conceptual banner. The "dominated" moment marks the era where the domination of labor still reigns. The idea of a "multilayered wholeness," or totality, points to the impossibility of totalizing the host of contemporaneous phenomena under the category of capitalism or, at the same time, toward the impossibility of reducing the historicity of our day to the conflict between capital and labor. The labor of capitalist production has never corresponded to the contemporaneity of the present, and its critique must leave space open for contradictions and noncontemporaneous hopes. The understanding of the social as a multilayered whole, as a unity that shows within itself a plurality of contradictions (each with its own temporality), allows us to imagine a revolutionary future. Without understanding noncontemporaneous contradictions, without the mobilization of their explosive

---

79   Ibid., 115.

power in the class struggle, the only future possible is that of reactionary politics of fascism. So, does Bloch consider all contradictions of equal importance? Are the struggles for the land and rootedness as decisive as class struggle?

On this point, it is clear that Bloch's answer is no. Viewed philosophically, the subordination of the contradictions linked to belonging (home, soil, nation) are manifest in the expression of their noncontemporaneity. To the extent that in the contemporary moment, certain contradictions are more contemporaneous than others, more alive, active, or explosive, these contradictions bring about more of the energy that can produce the new. However, in the philosophy of history, this subordination of the noncontemporaneous to the contemporaneous justifies how the workers' political superiority ends up leading to the proletariat. That the proletariat is made up of workers *and* the peasantry goes without saying. Different from Mariátegui, Bloch was always a fervent Bolshevik attached to the strategy of the alliance "of the proletariat with the impoverished peasants and the impoverished middle classes, under proletariat hegemony."[80] He writes about this "Triple Alliance":

> The genuinely contemporaneous contradiction has the duty of being concrete and total enough to detach the genuinely noncontemporaneous contradictions from reaction too and to bring them up to the tendency . . . But precisely no proletarian hegemony in the due Triple Alliance will succeed, above all no unfaded, unendangered one, without its also thoroughly "mastering" the substance of genuine noncontemporaneity and its heterogenous contradictions. By false consciousness and unfounded romanticism being everywhere expelled of course, but also by an understanding which is no *abstractly* omitting one taking in the subversive and utopian elements, the repressed matter of this not yet Past. It is certainly right to say that it is part of the nature of fascist ideology to incorporate the morbid resources of all cultural phases; but it is wrong to say only the morbid

---

80   Ibid., 113–14.

ones, namely as if the healthy ones were not accessible at all to the ideology of decay.[81]

This quote mixes the three fundamental themes of *Heritage of Our Times*. The synchronicity of the non-synchronous is not simply a critical theory of totality on the basis of which it is possible to conceptualize modernity; it also sets up the tactical alliance of employees, peasants, and workers under the leadership of workers. The theory of noncontemporaneity is the temporal basis of a political alliance and subordination within the Bolshevik Party. Finally, this tactical alliance can be realized only if it duly notes noncontemporaneity and takes "in the subversive and utopian elements" of noncontemporaneous contradictions. Effectively, this is a "domination" of the past and those who claim it for themselves: the peasantry's hold over the "soil," the impoverished middle classes of the "people," and all of the classes of the "family."

Any comparison between Mariátegui and Bloch should not diminish the difference between a Leninist philosopher who never gave up on worker hegemony and an indigenous thinker whose intervention begins by refusing this hegemony. But, in any case, it's striking to see how the theme of the multiplicity of temporalities is linked to the strategic question of alliances and the cultural question of hegemony. Hegemony can never be undone without the utopian, subversive element of history, the "repressed matter" of a past that is still present. Here, it is important to note an ambiguity that runs throughout my analysis of Bloch: on the one hand, utopia appears as a myth of a return to origins; on the other hand, it would seem to mark the invention of a future that has not yet come. How can the historical status of utopia be understood? Is it a past contradiction whose coming into being is still necessary (a historical tendency), or a future that waits to be invented (by the power of a subjectivity)?

On the one hand, utopia is the condition of the subjective possibility of a revolutionary act that is free to invent the future. It is caught in a political eschatology where the power of historical subjectivities is measured by their ability to anticipate and then actualize the future. On the

---

81   Ibid., 114.

other hand, utopia can only be, from the materialist point of view, the realization of necessary historical tendencies that are already present in the past. As Arno Münster has written, without an "ontological foundation of materialist order, the anticipations of the consciousness would be difficult to differentiate from illusions."[82] Bloch was trying to identify the ontological foundation of utopia through a naturalist perspective on matter.

Here, Mariátegui shares little, if anything, with Bloch. According to the latter, no revolutionary politics can do without an eschatological philosophy of history capable of integrating images of unrealized wishes of the past into the class struggle, namely, the attachment to the home, land, and nation. Rootedness appears as an unresolved utopian form of the Gemeinschaft, which communist politics must bear in mind. While it is clear that Mariátegui would have refused Bloch's tactical subordinations, at the same time the myth of the Andean attachment to the land gave to his thinking a utopian horizon. In both cases, the refusal of a racist politics (whether in regard to the indigenous communities or Jewish people) takes place, paradoxically, through the claiming of an attachment to the land. Can we ever claim land without this attachment catalyzing a racist identity politics? Can the reproduction of a relation between the group and its environment avoid the rootedness that would be the basis of an ethnicization of community?

Nationality, Ethnicity, and "Peruvianness"

Despite the differences of context that separate these two thinkers, Mariátegui and Bloch confronted a similar problem, namely, the racism of political organizations. They both tried to fight against the racism of their respective states and the blindness of socialists to their racism through a non-racial revalorization of the idea of belonging to the land. I have already shown how Bloch's theory of noncontemporaneity allowed

---

82   Arno Münster, *Ernst Bloch, messianisme et utopie. Introduction à une "phéno-ménologie" de la conscience anticipante* (Paris: PUF, 1989), 238.

him to resolve this apparent paradox. For Mariátegui, the defeat of the racism that victimized Andean Indians is an essential part of the struggle against colonization and its avatars in the modern nation-state. He writes about the "process of public instruction":

> Peruvian education, therefore, has a colonial rather than a national character. When the state refers to the Indians in its educational programs, it treats them as an inferior race; in this respect, the republic is no different from the viceroyalty.[83]

According to Mariátegui, the racism of the young republic reproduced the American colonial hierarchy between whites, Indians, and Blacks. Consequently, colonization was a projection of cultural domination of indigenous populations that expressed themselves in scholarly projects and in "state ideological apparatuses." This is because racial domination is not only cultural but also institutional. Between the Spanish viceroyalty and the creole independent republic, political institutions continued to discriminate. In every institutional form, colonial power was exercised through the demeaning of Indians, grouping them together in a preestablished racial hierarchy.[84] It's because of this racism that he supported a "national spirit" in the anticolonial struggle. Yet his ideological critique of the colonial character of the institutions of power was considered "racist" by the Comintern.[85] In other words, he was criticized for having introduced explicitly racist terms into problems that were deemed purely economic, while he was in fact looking to show how the racial problem was due to an economic problem of the "redistribution of agricultural property," a vein of thinking that allowed him to rethink the definition of the political community.[86]

---

83 Mariátegui, *Seven Interpretive Essays*, 84.

84 Aníbal Quijano, "Coloniality of Power, Eurocentrism, and Latin America," *Neplanta: Views from the South* 1, no. 3 (2000): 533–80.

85 Rollie Poppino, *International Communism in Latin America* (New York: Free Press of Glencoe, 1964), 56; cited in Paris, preface to Mariátegui, *Sept essais d'interprétation*, 28.

86 Mariátegui, *Seven Interpretive Essays*, 62.

Michael Löwy traces the trajectory of the Peruvian thinker, stating that "the national and cultural dimension of indigenism, suggested in his writing from 1927, seems to have disappeared in 1929."[87] "The Problem of Races in Latin America," the 1929 text to which Löwy refers, was destined for the first Communist Conference of Latin America, where the creation of an independent indigenous republic to foster the rights of Indians was debated. However, Mariátegui was very much opposed to this project: he refused to consider the indigenous question in Peru as a national question, that is to say, as a question about indigenous independence, and this was for two reasons.

A consideration of the economic situation of Indians made clear that the founding of this extremely poor modern Latin American nation-state would lead to the exploitation of the indigenous proletariat by a new indigenous bourgeoisie. He wanted to create a "Peruvianness" in which all minorities could participate.[88] The Peruvian character of its institutions would come from its Incan communist heritage, or the tradition of the division and collective use of the land that would define the new nationality or "ethnicity." "Without the Indian, Peruvianness is impossible," he writes, before adding a citation of Charles Maurras and Action Française: "Everything that is national is ours."[89] This strange reference to the royalist and anti-Semitic French organization suggests that we pause for a moment and consider Mariátegui's nationalist sensibility and the definition of racism he employed.

This definition mixed two ideas about race. In one way, he showed the retrograde nature of any historical analysis based on race. In 1929, he cited Bukharin to show how the problem of racial inequality did not emerge from the inferiority of "oppressed races" but from an economic and culturally inherited inequality:

---

87 Löwy, "L'Indigénisme," 19.
88 José Carlos Mariátegui, "El problema primario del Perú (1925)," *Peruanicemos al Perú. Obras Completas*, vol. 2 (Lima: Biblioteca Amauta, 1988), 41–6.
89 Ibid., 44.

This is a complete refutation of the theory of races. In sum, this theory reduces each race's characteristics to their "eternal nature." If this were the case, this "character" would certainly be expressed in the same manner in every era of history. What can we make of this? We can only state that this "nature" of races changes constantly with the conditions of their existence. These conditions are determined by the relations between society and nature, that is to say, by the state of productive forces. Consequently, the theory of races certainly cannot explain the conditions of social evolution.[90]

To the extent that the "nature" of a group varies according to the social and historical conditions in which the group evolves, his thinking does not lead to any form of politics of presupposed racial difference. Instead, it leads to a critique of theories about biological racism, which construct a hierarchy of peoples based on phenotypical differences—a hierarchy that legitimizes the colonial project of domination. But, in another way, Mariátegui did not deny outright the existence of "races," or of homogenous groups founded on such differences. These can become the object of a hierarchization on the basis of the colonial division of labor, as in the case of Peru. Here, the contemporary reader is sometimes shocked by Mariátegui's political vocabulary in those moments when a certain racism toward Blacks appears: "The black race, imported by the colonialists to augment their power over American indigeneity, passively filled its colonial role . . . Historically, the collapse of borders inside the proletariat permitted the improvement of the morality of blacks."[91]

It is indeed shocking to see here how all the effort he expended to separate race from cultural and educational questions concerning Peruvian Indians returns in the racial dogmatism he expressed regarding the Blacks of the country. The belief in a homogenous and passive Black mass that is both ignorant and immoral relies on the imaginary

---

90 Mariátegui, "El problema de las razas en la America Latina," in *Ideología y política*, 30.

91 Ibid., 27–8.

of slavery perpetuated by European colonists who participated in the slave trade. It's necessary, then, to ask ourselves whether his claim to Peruvian nationalism based on communist land use does not lead back to a racialization of the social groups that participate in citizenship in differing ways. Calling for nationalism in terms that weren't that dissimilar from those of anti-Semitic European social formations, Mariátegui developed a contradictory anticolonial strain of thought: on the one hand, he urged the decolonization of the institutions of state power; on the other hand, he accepted the cultural heritage of a racial hierarchy based on the division of labor, while justifying the notion of nationality based on a new definition of ethnicity. However, we know how racism is historically linked to attempts to define an ethnically pure nation.

It is nevertheless possible to propose a reading of this "communism of rootedness" in line with Bloch, which would argue that Mariátegui was closer to Sorel's revolutionary syndicalism than to Maurras's anti-Semitism, which, in fact, Mariátegui criticized elsewhere.[92] For Mariátegui, there would be no way forward for a communist movement in Peru without the construction of an identity in which the "nationalists and liberal bourgeois democrats" had invested themselves.[93] Similar to how Bloch believed that the communist movement had to rid noncontemporaneous contradictions from reactionary politics, Mariátegui believed, heeding Sorel's call, that the socialist movement had to take back nationality from the nationalists. To claim belonging to a pluriethnic nationality is based on the heritage of the collective property of lands and common uses of the land that defined the structure of productive relations in Andean agrarian communities. Colonization led to a hierarchization of the white, Indian, Creole, and Black populations according to their role in the relations of production and exchange. Thus, for Mariátegui, Incan communism was intended to be not just a specific

---

92   José Carlos Mariátegui, "'L'action française,' Charles Maurras, Léon Daudet," December 15, 1926, and "El hombre y el mito," in *El Alma Matinal y otras estaciones del hombre de hoy. Obras Completas*, vol. 3 (Lima: Biblioteca Amauta).

93   Mariátegui, "El problema de las razas," 44.

mode of production but the invention of the national myth that would inspire the urban proletariat to struggle against the bourgeoisie and the colonial institutions of power. Here, we can find three ways in which Mariátegui's thinking resembled Sorel's.

First, Mariátegui discovered in Sorel's work a mythical and spiritual strain of thought that gave an important place to faith in the revolutionary act and that revalorized religion in social practices.[94] It was this revolutionary enthusiasm that first attracted Mariátegui to Sorel. Second, it is incontestable that Mariátegui was aware of Sorel's proximity to French royalist, anti-Semitic groups.[95] It's clear that the idea of Peruvianness that would serve as the mortar for a national communism is not entirely unconnected to the nationalist aspirations of the revolutionary French syndicalist. But, third, we can see that it was not so much the relation between ethnicity and nationality that garnered Mariátegui's attention as the territorial and environmental inscription of forms of political organization. As Alice Ingold has written, Sorel was an inspector in the Department of Roads and Bridges, and his socialist philosophy retained traces of thinking formed while in contact with regional cooperative landowner groups interested in the administration of rivers.[96] Mariátegui often cited *Reflections on Violence* and the *Social Foundations of Contemporary Economics*; it's less clear whether he had read *Materials for a Theory of the Proletariat*, where Sorel's emphasis on cooperation

---

94   Ibid., 22–3.

95   Everyone today acknowledges Sorel's anti-Semitism. But interpretations vary about its breadth, longevity, and radical nature. For Shlomo Sand, it was a flatulent and superficial anti-Semitism, something characteristic of his time rather than his thought, while for Zeev Sternell, he became one of the fathers of fascism and of this new alliance between socialist thought and nationalism. See Shlomo Sand, "Sorel, les Juifs et l'antisémitisme," *Mil neuf cent. Revue d'histoire intellectuelle (Cahiers Georges Sorel)* 2 (1984): 7–36; and Zeev Sternhell, *Neither Right nor Left: Fascist Ideology in France*, trans. David Maisel (Princeton, NJ: Princeton University Press, 1995).

96   Alice Ingold, "Terres et eaux entre coutume, police et droit au XIXe siècle. Solidarisme écologique ou solidarités matérielles?," *Tracés. Revue de Sciences humaines* 33 (2017): 97–126; Georges Sorel, *Materials for a Theory of the Proletariat* (London: Routledge, 1987).

was in evidence.[97] It's highly likely, however, that he found in Sorel's thinking about regional organizations an echo of his own thinking on the role of the Andean community in the development of socialism.[98] Peruvian nationality and Incan ethnicity played an ideological role consisting of uniting all of the subdivisions of the proletariat in the same struggle against the colonial bourgeoisie and the creole republic. Evidently, the problem was that this class struggle was doubly "encoded" by the necessity of constituting a pluri-ethnic, national identity. It was to avoid an overly ethnic-based struggle for emancipation that Mariátegui had interpreted the "Indian problem" as a "problem of the land." Here, nationality does not have the bourgeois meaning of a trans-class ideology that would unite social groups whose interests are antagonistic (proletarians and capitalists) within one imagined community. Instead, it is the catalyst of a postcolonial hegemony of oppressed groups that could unite, despite their social and racial differences, against the exploiting classes. It's not the union of proletarians and national capitalists against the foreigner, but the community of proletarians, peasants, slaves, indigenous peoples, and Blacks against the capitalists. Nationality is defined by the common belonging to the land which had been taken from them by dominant groups.

From Nation to Land: Anti-Semitism and the Indigenous Question

"The idea that the indigenous problem is an ethnic problem is not worthy of being discussed," Mariátegui wrote in 1929.[99] Following his work in

---

97 Georges Sorel, *Reflections on Violence*, trans. T. E. Hulme (London: George Allen & Unwin, 1916); Georges Sorel, *Social Foundations of Contemporary Economics*, trans. John L. Stanley (New York: Routledge, 1984), and *Materials for a Theory of the Proletariat*, trans. John L. Stanley, in *Essays in Socialism and Philosophy* (New York: Routledge, 1987).

98 Mariátegui wrote about the cooperatives developed by Sorel in "El porvenir de la cooperativas," in *Ideología y política*.

99 Mariátegui, "El problema de las razas," 26.

Seven Interpretive Essays, the Peruvian writer asserted here that the problem of indigenous peoples was not "determined by race but by economics and politics."[100] Based on this, it would be a mistake to say that he denied the existence of racial hierarchies; rather, his point was that racism, as a hierarchy founded on the idea of a phenotypical or cultural homogeneity of social groups, was based ultimately on forms of economic exploitation and relations of political domination: social, economic, and political relations determine racial hierarchies. Without a doubt, we see that Mariátegui was arguing against nineteenth-century biological theories of racism. What explains the exploited lives of Indians is their place in the relations of production and in political institutions. As they no longer own land but are also not wage laborers, they are effectively serfs or slaves:

> Therefore, they sought to convert to mining a people who had been essentially agricultural under the Inca and even before, and they ended by having to subject the Indian to the harsh law of slavery. Agricultural labor, under a naturally feudal system, would have made the Indian a serf bound to the land. Labor in mines and cities was to turn him into a slave. With the *mita*, the Spaniards established a system of forced labor and uprooted the Indian from his soil and his customs.[101]

The racial hierarchy of Peru is determined by the relations of production: Black slaves work in the mines, Indians work in the latifundia as forced labor, creoles own businesses, and whites are the owners of the plantations and manage the institutions of power. It was the relation to the land and the division of labor that determined for Mariátegui the position of racial hierarchies.[102] Mariátegui wrote, "It's logical that they demand the return of all the lands that they could cultivate."[103] The gap between

---

100   Ibid., 31.
101   Mariátegui, *Seven Interpretive Essays*, 54.
102   Mariátegui, "El problema de las razas," 21.
103   Ibid., 71.

national and cultural discourse in 1927 and the economic emphasis of 1929 is explained by circumstantial and political reasons in the first case (the struggle against the Comintern) and by theoretical reasons in the latter case: racialization is an effect of the labor division. Again, the economic theory of racism enters into contradiction with the ideological positions on the point of Blacks. This theory of racism is the largest difference between Bloch and Mariátegui.

Bloch's philosophy shares with Mariátegui's thinking the same concern about fighting against forms of racism that prevent the founding of a victorious socialist movement. In contrast to the chauvinism of communist parties, they were looking to understand the causes of anti-Semitism and anti-indigenous racism. The original theory of noncontemporaneity held that anti-Semitism expressed only an objectively contemporary contradiction, since Bloch believed that anti-Semitism's subjective dimensions were determined by elements of a noncontemporaneous contradiction (the attachment to the *German soil* as catalyst for the identity of a *nation* through the transmission of the rights of inheritance in the order of the *family and bloodline*). In other words, anti-Semitism was no longer linked only to the economic structure of relations of production, but also to the political persistence of the effects of an inherited structure integrated into the social whole. Bloch looked to avoid economic simplification in the analysis of anti-Semitism and to understand the political autonomy of this phenomenon.

We see here how an understanding of how Mariátegui fit into the context of his times is important for appreciating his work: during his time, racial hierarchies were still deeply ingrained in the very structure of the relations of production. This is why his political project was that of a return to a mythical original unity of the peasantry and the land, a foundation of a pluri-ethnic national community incarnated as Incan communism. While, for Mariátegui, agrarian and indigenous communism was the utopian expression of a struggle against bourgeois exploitation and colonial-racial domination, Bloch was, rather, preoccupied with the ability of a principally urban and worker movement to integrate rural utopian elements so as to encourage the peasant masses to join. Their respective intellectual projects bear witness to a materialist attention to the particularity of economic situations and to the non-dogmatic desire to integrate the subaltern fringes of the proletariat into the class struggle. In Germany, the abandonment of the peasantry and the middle classes reduced to the proletariat signaled a victory for fascism. Because of their inability to control the keywords "home," "soil," and "nation," the communists alienated parts of the population, thereby paving the way for the victory of reactionary forces. Inversely, in Peru, indigenous peoples were only able to score victories over the racist-colonial institutions of white power when they were able to show that their problem was related to the land, which is to say, to private property and the means of subsistence.

Many differences can be found between Bloch's attempt to base Bolshevism on a theory of historical noncontemporaneity and Mariátegui's project for an indigenous agrarian Marxism inspired by the myth of Incan communism. However, the effort to locate in the past the utopian sources for an agrarian communism is linked to a certain tendency of historical materialism that we might call "practical naturalism."

In both, we see how an attachment to the land becomes concretized in political practice, and how this practice is founded on the material possi-bility of change and the images of contemporary desires glimpsed in the heritage of the past. The essential part of this eschatological current of historical materialism is the place accorded to belief—including reli-gious belief—in the origin stories of unity and belonging. While we should not "divide people into revolutionary or conversative types, but as people of great or little imagination," nevertheless the historical process presupposes a "heroic creation."[104] Separate from a modernizing and productivist materialism, these naturalist eschatologies bear witness to the need to take seriously the affective attachment to the land, the practical power of faith, and the demand for territorial autonomy in the class struggle.

Affective and mystical attachment to the land produces contradictory effects in contemporary political speech. On the one hand, it leads

---

104   Mariátegui, *El alma*, 39; Mariátegui, "Aniversario," 249.

environmental organizations to incorporate non-modern cosmologies. This allows them to go beyond a biocentric vision of conservation founded on the protection of certain wild species (to the exclusion of humans) and thus to produce an ecocentricism based on the protection of the relations of ecosystems (relations that duly incorporate humans and non-humans). On the other hand, the revalorization of the attachment to the land gives rise, at times, to rather naive forms of fetishization and the folklorization of autochthonous communities reputed to be "closer to nature." Animism no longer seems like a specific historical form of the socialization of the real; instead, it's naturalized, to the point of reproducing the colonial image of non-Western collectivities with their inherent relations to nature.

The juridical personification of the Whanganui River in New Zealand is a good example in contemporary thought of this ambivalence of an "animist becoming."[105] On March 15, 2017, the New Zealand Parliament recognized the Whanganui River as a living entity and granted it juridical status. The technical difficulty of this acknowledgement consisted of how to incorporate Maori claims in Common Law. The Maori wanted to protect the ecological balance of the river and to receive acknowledgement of their right to a certain degree of political autonomy. The agreement merged a philosophy on natural resources defined as a common good with aspects of animist cosmology; and it transformed the governance of the river, creating an anthropomorphized character, Te Awa Tupua (the river), who is represented by two physical people, the first named by the New Zealand government, the other by the Iwi people. These two representatives together are an administrative organism called Te Pou Tupua. This entity benefits from the aid of two committees. The first is composed of tribal members and representatives of local authorities; the other is tasked with the management of the river over the long haul and is made up of representatives for those using the river. The agreement publicly acknowledges animist, Maori, cosmological elements; aims for the careful management of natural resources by

---

105   Marie-Angèle Hermitte, "Artificialisation de la nature et droit(s) du vivant," in Philippe Descola, ed., *Les Natures en question* (Paris: Odile Jacob, 2018), 173.

environmental institutions that will organize governance over the river (inspired by economist Elinor Ostrom's theory of common goods); and prevents the river from being owned privately. Here, animism is tied to a definition of life in which "the interiorities of humans and non-humans have enough common parts and common interests for all beings to be subject to the law, whatever differences may exist in their physical characteristics."[106] A similar decision occurred in Nainital, India, in March 2017 when the High Court of Uttarakhand gave juridical status to the Ganges and Yamuna rivers. While the contents and the legal foundation of each case differ greatly, these decisions bear witness to efforts to grant rights to nature as a living subject, and so to consecrate elements of animist cosmology in the laws of modern nation-states.

Yet, the idea that non-modern cosmologies would be consecrated in the language of Western law does not come without a series of questions about the nature and scope of the translation of these cosmologies. Does this becoming-animist of modern law have a corollary for animist ontologies—a becoming-naturalist? Might the naturalization of animism correspond to a new Western imperialism under the peaceful auspices of environmental law? Should we be wary, taking up the formulation of Pablo Solón, of introducing a "concept of 'rights' [that] is a construction coming from outside the indigenous context?"[107]

For my part, I take the interlacing of modern law with elements of animist cosmologies as the sign that the desire to escape from naturalism is politically untenable. There are phenomena of ontological hybridization characteristic of postcolonial situations all around us, through which new transnational strategies might emerge. These cosmologies do not exist independently of property relations that define forms of attachment to the land. We cannot reduce destructive practices to symbolic systems that legitimize them. It's true that one type of mechanical naturalism provided the ideology for the extractivist logic of capitalism, which it used to justify the pillaging of the earth and the exploitation of

---

106   Ibid., 173.

107   Pablo Solón, "Les Droits de la Terre Mère," in *Des droits pour la nature* (Paris: Les Éditions Utopia, 2016), 63.

labor. But this mechanism was only one among many forms of naturalism. What cosmologies do we need to reformulate a model of collective ownership that authorizes sustainable uses of the land? Our ways of identifying the world must take into account the power of nonhuman realities to act in social history. Yet, it's my view that it's not necessary to turn away from naturalism per se in order to conceive of cosmologies that are more respectful of nonhuman worlds.

Conclusion
For a Communism of Life

Look, the origin of usury, theft and robbery lies with our lords and princes, who treat all creatures as their possessions: the fish in the water, the birds in the air, the plants on the earth—everything must be theirs.
—Thomas Müntzer, "Highly Provoked Vindication," trans. Andy Drummond

In his book *Down to Earth*, Bruno Latour speculated on how politics could be adapted for the Anthropocene. One answer emerged: the communism of life.

A *living communism* against those who would like to reduce it to the outmoded experience of Soviet productivism, but also against the dogmatic image of a communism frozen in time with nothing to say to us now and whose mention could only return us to dogma and cliché: "Communism is . . . not a *state of affairs* which is to be established, an *ideal* to which reality [will] have to adjust itself. We call communism the *real* movement which abolishes the present state of things."[1] Moving forward, the eradication of the conditions that create human misery and

---

1 Friedrich Engels and Karl Marx, *The German Ideology*, trans. William Lough (Moscow: Progress Publishers, 1976), 57.

suffering will be our goal; our focus will be turned to ending the exploitation of nature and labor and bringing about a living relation to the earth. This is true in the case of Standing Rock and in the many decolonial struggles of indigenous peoples, and it is also true in the *zones à défendre*, particularly at Notre-Dame-des-Landes. A living communism is attentive to the immanent forms of the real movement of the eradication of value; it cannot rest content with repeating the outmoded political programs of bygone worlds.

A *communism of living labor* against capital. Living labor is the activity of humans who organize their relations to materiality while producing the conditions of their existence. Labor is the "process between man and nature, a process by which man, through his own actions, mediates, regulates and controls the metabolism between himself and nature. He confronts the materials of nature as a force of nature."[2] A communism of living labor is of vital importance because it reproduces the material conditions of human life and transforms the individuals who engage in it. In capitalism, living labor is the activity by which value is created—a type of creation often mediated by machines and tools that are a part of "dead labor." To wrest living labor from the throes of capital in order to produce a less pathological unity of humans and Earth is how communism will help us exit the Capitalocene. The communism of living labor aims at the collective reappropriation of the material conditions of subsistence. Its first goal is, thus, to take back the land, and to put an end to its capitalist appropriation.

A *communism of life* against death. Disaster capitalism habituates us to the destruction of the conditions of life, to the mass extinction of species, and to the widespread upending of ecosystems. A communist politics can no longer serve only human interests, if only because our vital interests imply the stability and well-being of biological communities. Moving forward, it will be necessary to include in the communist agenda the defense of multispecies commons, since "these commons that do not belong to anyone are of course multi-purposed

---

2 Karl Marx, *Capital: A Critique of Political Economy*, trans. Ben Fowkes (Harmondsworth: Penguin, 1976), 284.

resources—forests, fields, pastureland, rivers, wetlands, aquifers, but also urban parks, unused land and gardens—allowing humans to live without having to depend continually on the market."[3] The communism of life is multispecific: it aims for the subsistence of human and non-human collectivities.

To place life at the center of a communist politics means reforming its cosmology based on renewed naturalism. To the extent that environments are made up of many species, natures are co-productions between humans and non-humans. To speak of the generative power of natural beings, we can use the phrase the "autonomy of nature." In living beings, there is an agency independent of the cultural codification through which we perceive it. Moreover, the social history of nature modifies the conditions of the ecological history of societies. In speaking of a heteronomous history of nature, I must insist on emphasizing capitalism's power of disruption and destruction. This social history is nothing other than a theory of the material transformations of natural environments. Natures always reveal themselves to us through situated cultural conditions. Their manifestations are apparent only through the intermediary of norms determined in specific contexts. This is why historical naturalism (nature has a social history and societies have a natural history) is also cultural naturalism, that is, a theory of the aesthetic conditions of the manifestations of natures. The context is produced by the history of the struggles for the appropriation of nature and labor. Because natures have political histories, they are the fodder for conceptual disagreements. Political struggles concerning ways of using the earth are based on ontological conflicts over the possible meanings of naturalness. Historical multi-naturalism allows us to conceive of the autonomy, historicity, and the multiplicity of natures.

Our perceptions of life become more sensitive to its powers to act and to constitute worlds. We no longer notice only that all forms of life are affected by our actions, but now we also notice their capacity to affect

---

3   Léna Balaud and Antoine Chopot, *Nous ne sommes pas seuls. Politique des soulèvements terrestres* (Paris: Seuil, 2021), 369.

other objective beings: plants, like Japanese knotweed or amaranth, which colonize entire ecosystems which had previously been rendered impoverished or fragile by massive transformations.[4] This renewed attention to non-human beings defines the political ecology of the Capitalocene. But the communism of life cannot rest satisfied with the cosmological transformation of sensibilities; it must intervene in a strategic manner in political organizations capable of dramatically changing our relations to materiality.

With climate change underway, three political scenarios emerge as possibilities. In the first, the most tragic, we await the catastrophe that will return us to the ethical conditions of a more sober life (collapsology), that is, a life entirely stripped of the last traces of civilization (survivalism). Here, we envision a global collapse. The fear of certain fringes of the proletariat of the North is that the precarity of their subsistence conditions will increase further, and that the economic-political institutions that have guaranteed them a decent standard of living for several decades will disappear. This scenario also expresses a legitimate fear of the collapse of civilization into barbarity: the weakening functionality of resource-management systems could provoke the disappearance of ethical norms of social life, leading to civil war. It is not at all absurd to imagine such scenarios; rather, what is absurd is to pretend that they are not already taking place in many nation-states brought to their knees by economic and political crises or imploding under imperialist wars. The collapse of nation-states and the institutions that assure the minimal conditions of social reproduction characterizes the "idyllic proceedings" of the accumulation of capital, which "has the globe as its battlefield."[5] And other collapses are taking place in the here and now, beginning with that of global biodiversity. In the countries of the North, the fear of collapse is also tied to the fear of decline and the loss of geopolitical power which would mean that the nations of the North would suffer the same fate as countries subjected to colonial-imperial predations. These apocalyptic scenarios risk reinforcing the politics of borders

---

4 Ibid., 7–10.
5 Marx, *Capital*, 915.

and border control, and exploiting the rhetoric of resource and land scarcity.

The second scenario bases its hopes on technological innovations that would save us from the disasters that the machines of the past several centuries have produced; this is the solution of geoengineering led by green capitalism.[6] To replace polluting fossil fuel use, certain businesses are transitioning to nuclear energy. Yet, green capitalism "solves" its crises only by displacing the problem: it goes from a climate crisis brought on by fossil fuel use to a crisis due to atomic energy, where the problem of waste is added to the ongoing possibility of nuclear catastrophe. This energy is at once expensive and much slower to put in place than renewable energies; it poses many problems in terms of the extraction of uranium and the subterranean storage of waste.[7] The scenario by which technological innovation would foster ecological solutions is dubious at best (just like plans to reverse-engineer a cooler planet through global engineering feats). To be sure, in this scenario, productivism is not scrutinized, and the idea that human well-being is dependent on our ability to keep producing more material and immaterial goods continues unchanged. Without a significant and immediate reduction in the production of goods, there's no hope to limit ecological harm, pollution, and waste. It is arithmetically impossible to produce more goods with fewer resources, while emitting less pollution and creating no post-consumption by-products. Moreover, technological innovation all too often evades the deliberative procedures of democracy.

Green capitalism is backed by all the ideologues of "greenwashing" who promise that the market has the technical means of continuing to mass-produce while encouraging a rapid ecological transition. They

---

6   Daniel Tanuro, *Green Capitalism: Why It Can't* Work, tr. unknown (Halifax: Fernwood, 2014).

7   On the global economics of uranium and the anti-democratic character of nuclear technologies, please see the remarkable work of Gabrielle Hecht in *The Radiance of France: Nuclear Power and National Identity after World War II* (Boston: MIT Press, 2000), and *Being Nuclear: Africans and the Global Uranium Trade* (Boston: MIT Press, 2012).

pretend that data points about profit in new sectors of the global market provide a lasting solution. They speak of staving off two threats to profit: the first is the desire of ethical consumers to lessen the impact of their consumption on the planet; the second is the absence of the potential of capitalization in many sectors of production. At every juncture where we find, for example, the means of reintroducing waste into the market cycle, there are businesses that make new profits from what had been previously without value. But technological innovations cannot guarantee a lasting solution, since they only aim at new forms of production. The plans for reinventing the capitalist economy that the "green growth" ideal promises mask the fundamental fact that the accumulation of value presupposes a production of goods that necessitates the extraction of ever more biophysical resources. The labels "organic" and "eco-district" that aim at improving the health of people and luring people to towns are evidence of this cosmetic acceptability: we can farm without herbicides and pesticides, but for the costs to remain acceptable to the majority of consumers, production must take place in often-deplorable working conditions at a distance of some thousands of kilometers from the places of consumption, with a very heavy carbon footprint. We can continue to build cities and pave streets, just as long as a couple plants are added to lend a superficial gloss of greenery. The cosmetic hypocrisy of "greenwashing" is limitless.

The third scenario is for state-based regulation of harmful polluting practices. This is advocated either by democratic consensus, when the imaginary of socioecology follows that of social democracy; or by authoritarianism or green nationalism, when it becomes a talking point of the far right. It's clear that all forms of state-based regulation will not work politically. The efforts to maintain ecological reforms within democracy's horizon are incomparably more desirable than any ethnonationalist politics of retrenchment. Whatever their actual effect may be, they at least aim for respecting the rights and the dignity of collectivities. On the opposite end of the spectrum, there are "green nationalisms" and their protectionist and identitarian administration of disasters. They construct borders that protect landscapes and populations deemed legitimate, while they plow through foreign natures and peoples with policies of unrestrained appropriation. While wanting to preserve environments through population controls (the imposition of borders and the idea of nativism), neo-Malthusian ecologies favor the idea of an ethno-racial purity within the political community. Incumbent in this politics is the idea that the population is excessive and its growth must be limited. Here, green ethnonationalism resembles Xi Jinping's China.[8]

From the perspective of an energy transition, the Chinese president announced on September 22, 2020, that the state was aiming to be carbon neutral by 2060. In becoming the first large capitalist power to abide by the Paris Climate Accord, China would gain moral prestige and climate credibility in ecological circles. Economically speaking, the People's Republic would hope to become a global leader in the transition from fossil fuels to renewable and nuclear energies. But we should harbor no illusions. This energy program would fuel an enormous relaunch of the Chinese economy. If we take them at their word, then these public statements are more than mere propaganda; they forecast the replacement of the fossil fuel motors that enable the production and transportation of goods. A greenwashing project on a massive scale would assure an enormous market for energy production (primitive, nuclear, and renewable capital) and industry. China would become the technological cutting edge of energy and "green combustion," reinforcing its status as the good climate actor and the principal center for ecologically sound global capitalism. In England, the transition from coal to gas in the 1910s is usually explained by the political struggle that was destined to take power from miners and railway workers.[9] Similar tactics are no doubt at play in the Chinese energy transition. Politically speaking, it's not at all clear that ethnonationalists are climate deniers, by and large. While fascism was historically tied to a fossil fuel economy whose interests it protected, it is entirely possible that modern nation-states might move to

---

8   Pierre Charbonnier, "Le tourant réaliste de l'écologie politique. Pourquoi les écologistes doivent apprendre à parler le langage de la géopolitique," *Le Grand Continent*, September 30, 2020.

9   Timothy Mitchell, *Carbon Democracy: Political Power in the Age of Oil* (London: Verso, 2013).

develop nationalist politics and plans for green capitalism.[10] It's a safe bet that capital would try to play both sides: the politics of climate deniers would exist to satisfy the interests of fossil fuel capitalism; and the search for new profits in green sectors of the economy would be lucrative as well. This energy transition is not incompatible (in theory) with strong nationalism, as the racist and concentration-camp-like politics against the Uighurs makes clear. Green nationalisms reinforce the power of the state founded on the basis of a trans-class hegemonic bloc that wants to preserve the eternal landscape of the nation and the racial homogeneity of the community. The example of China shows that the scenarios of state regulation and green capitalism often reinforce each other.

Social ecology responds to different dynamics. As Naomi Klein has shown regarding the Green New Deal, social ecology uses an ecological regulation of the economy to spur the politics of social and climate justice.[11] It asks for the federal government to invest broadly in a green economy. While this promotes an economic policy that is commendable from the perspective of social and climate justice, it faces three obstacles: the multidimensional character of a crisis that is not limited to the energy sector; the productivism that subtends everything; and the inegalitarian character (between North and South) of an ecological transition that presupposes state investment of a considerable amount of money. The Green New Deal aims to "decarbonize" production (as do similar European projects), which is to say, to leave the fossil fuel economy behind, while greatly expanding renewable energy applications. In short, the goal is to substitute a large-scale production apparatus for goods that is less polluting than a technological mode of production that is a heavy emitter of greenhouse gases. This plan demands a capitalist restructuring of production across all sectors of the economy. It is true that, as it is imagined today, this plan for growth aims to create jobs and to assure a certain social justice through the modality of

---

10   Zetkin Collective and Andreas Malm, *White Skin, Black Fuel: On the Danger of Fossil Fascism* (London: Verso, 2021).

11   Naomi Klein, *On Fire: The (Burning) Case for a Green New Deal* (New York: Simon & Schuster, 2019).

redistribution. But because it does not challenge the underlying productivism, that is, the necessity of increasing production to grow profits, it can only lead to an enormous use of natural resources (sand for concrete, minerals for electronic parts, uranium for electricity). At the end of the consumer chain, this use of materials leads to the stockpiling of construction waste and spent nuclear fuel. In short, these Green New Deals projects of the North American left and the social democratic European states can only be put in place by nation-states with the means to finance them. As one of its proponents stated to the United Nations Conference on Trade and Development, "Direct credit controls become unfashionable in the era of 'efficient markets,'" and so it's necessary to imagine "incentives (e.g. placing government deposits) and disincentives (e.g. portfolio restrictions)" in order to push credit toward the most productive investment opportunities.[12] In short, the liberal democratic version of the Green New Deal intends to create not a politics of a definancialization of the economy but only a reorientation of production that would incite capital markets to finance the green sector. The number of jobs created would hardly make up for the fact that no thought has been given to the labor conditions in these sectors. On this point, we can scarcely see how this economic program would apply to other nation-states beyond the principal powers (the US, Europe, China, and Japan). Only those with borrowing power, that is, the ability to negotiate the structure of their debts, would be able to envisage financing such a program. Support for climate justice still risks being a vain effort limited to elite nations.

But the impact of state regulation will remain limited if the underlying problem of the nation-state's role in the ecological reproduction of class relations is not dealt with. As is commonly proposed, this scenario will moderate only the most destructive tendencies of technology and the global market. Without a general transformation of the structure of property, it is difficult to imagine that institutional regulations will lead to anything other than a simple reorientation of the productivist

---

12   Richard Kozul-Wright, "How to Finance a Global Green New Deal," LSE: Sustainable Finance Leadership Series, November 6, 2019, lse.ac.uk.

economy and the establishment of a dispositif of a posteriori financial compensation for the most disruptive uses.

The existential threat, the technological solution of geoengineering, and the state-based project of ecological regulation and collapse: each scenario touches upon a sliver of reality. (Multiple collapses have already taken place; certain problems have technological solutions; climate regulation is a necessity.) But all are relatively inconsequential insomuch as they skirt the real problem: the causes of the environmental catastrophe are written into the class structure of capitalism. The destruction of nature is the historical result of a mode of production geared for profit by the sale of commodities produced by exploited workers. At each moment in the economic cycle, capital ravages the earth: the extraction of biophysical resources depletes natural resources, production emits industrial and agricultural pollutants, the circulation of goods uses a transportation network that relies on fossil fuel consumption, and consumerism produces a world where trash piles up in dumps that grow higher every day. This destructive dynamic of capital has a clear historical trajectory: it's a system of the general appropriation of the natural conditions of subsistence. Moreover, the appropriation of natures is synonymous with the exploitation of labor by capital: there is no extraction of coal or gold without miners; there are no strawberries in the supermarket without seasonal migrant laborers. As Marx wrote in 1867,

> [All] progress in capitalist agriculture is a progress in the art, not only of robbing the worker, but of robbing the soil; all progress in increasing the fertility of the soil at a given time is a progress towards ruining the more longlasting sources of that fertility . . . Capitalist production, therefore, only develops the techniques and the degree of combination of the social process of production by simultaneously undermining the original sources of all wealth—the soil and the worker.[13]

Humans and non-humans have a common problem: capitalism is a world-ecology that dispossesses life from access to its conditions

---

13   Marx, *Capital*, 638.

of reproduction. Far from being irrelevant in face of the new conditions of our ecological crisis, the historical call to action of communism—the abolition of private property—is more urgent than ever.

The communism of life is not only a cosmological change; it strives for the reappropriation of the conditions of subsistence against capitalist monopolization. It brings with it choices. To the extent that the destruction of nature presupposes an exploitation of human labor (paid or unpaid), it is impossible to imagine the preservation of the biosphere without pursuing universal social emancipation. The traditional question of the labor movement is asked again in new ways: What are the means for the proletariat of all life forms to abolish value? It's a cliché to say that labor strategies will become polarized around a schematic opposition between those wishing to take control of state power and the chaotic forces of struggle itself, or between organization and autonomy. While the communist movement favors the seizure of state power, anarchist movements would prefer the autonomy of collectivities. But this either-or is a caricature: the Bolsheviks in 1917 didn't "seize" the bourgeois state; they helped bring about the collapse of existing structures and the establishment of new institutions. As the entire globe faces climate change, it is increasingly hard to imagine that the wholesale transformation of the material infrastructure of social life could be initiated exclusively from outside the nation-state: coercive measures to limit pollution, the revolution in agrarian production, and the banning of genetically modified organisms all presuppose forms of ecological and public health planning that go far beyond the capacity of grassroots freedom struggles to implement. While reliance upon the state to help inaugurate ecological transition appears necessary in order to limit the power of capitalists, at the same time, we know that the way nation-states put to use their territorial resources beyond all natural cycles of sustainability is in fact one of the leading causes of the ecological crisis. Witness, for example, the carbon footprint of armies. It is important, then, to be able to "live inside the disturbance," and to defend ecological action against power grabs, so long as we remember it must be directed toward the collapse of the modern nation-state.[14] Modern nation-states are not all monolithic blocs that service the bourgeoisie, but they guarantee the reproduction of class relations, and they aim at maintaining them over time. While we might like to take up again the ecological thinking of the Bolsheviks, we must also remember what Lenin wrote, quoting Marx, in *The State and Revolution*: "All revolutions perfected this machine instead of smashing it."[15] The communism of life must rely for the time being on the strategy of "dual power" in the Anthropocene.

Theorized by the 1917 revolutionaries, dual power is a political anomaly: the coexistence of a temporary government inherited from the tsarist state but elected by the Duma and various governance boards. In the worker soviets or soldier assemblies, elected representatives stood in for the proletariat and made important decisions about the management of the commune, factory, and regiment. They sent delegates to the Central Committee of Soviets. The problem is no longer knowing whether to take power over from the state or not, but knowing how to organize the transition, with which means, and according to which power relations. The power of the soviets came from their ability to abolish previous social structures. Peasants dressed as soldiers shot officers so as to take over military power, and the administration of production was managed by worker delegates. Therefore, the soviets not only constituted a novel form of government alongside central power, but deeply modified two aspects of revolutionary tactics. First, they helped bring about the end of political institutions that supported class domination (beginning with the military and the factory). Second, they revoked the capitalist division of economics and politics. The political organization of labor was exercised at the sites of production. The delegates were under the control of the masses who modified the relations of power by direct action. The armed people, organized in small administrative bodies, were much

---

14   Donna Haraway, *Staying with the Trouble: Making Kin in the Chthulucene* (Durham, NC: Duke University Press, 2016).

15   Vladimir I. Lenin, *The State and Revolution*, ed. and trans. R. Service (London: Penguin, 1992), 26.

more powerful than the temporary government weakened by the Duma and its parliamentary decrees. In April 1917, Lenin considered the *structural* opposition between the soviets and the central government as the key that could lead toward a revolutionary transition. Without that structural opposition, the bourgeois elements within the inherited governmental structure might short-circuit the process. Dual power was the new political contradiction of revolutionary times: conflicts *within* the progressivist forces would determine the pace of the revolution. It was not the state *or* the soviets, but the soviets *in* and *against* the state. The soviets had the power to force the provisional government to take revolutionary measures. Though quickly abandoned for the strategy of a dictatorship of the proletariat organized by the vanguard, dual power appeared between February and October 1917 as a governmental form comparable in structure to the Paris Commune, where worker self-organization existed at the same time as the bourgeois state. But this incipient moment of proletariat power came after lengthy organizational work and the creation of worker culture. Since 1905, the soviets had long formed the political identity of revolutionary Russians. They constituted a form of political autonomy in relation to the state institutions and parties (including the Bolsheviks) and a new power that would be deployed at the sites of production to replace previous political structures. While, for Lenin, dual power was only possible in a moment of transition defined by the crisis of state institutions, it is still useful to reimagine its significance for the Anthropocene. How could dual power be useful from an ecological point of view?

The ecological crisis is a crisis of subsistence. Based on depriving people of the necessary conditions of reproduction, capital grows while accumulating every possible form of wealth. Therefore, the struggles for decent living conditions and for food and health autonomy come to have, in themselves, a revolutionary dimension. They become the strategic sites of the combat against capital. According to Fredric Jameson, the Black Panthers Party offered food, waste management services, and health coverage to the community under their purview; they offered to an oppressed population what the segregationist nation-state did not.

This has been the same for Hamas in our time. Practical help on a daily basis guarantees the conditions of social reproduction. At the same time, the ecological fight against capital must be balanced against the importance of the autonomy of our means of subsistence. This "dual biopower" is being realized today in ecological struggles that create new supply chains or that take over territory.[16] In terms of the supply chain, there are the examples of the mutual-aid networks of the *gilets jaunes* (yellow vests), as well as community food redistribution initiatives. In terms of the second, there are the *zones à défendre* and, more generally, disputed lands that, sheltering multispecies commons, provide the means of survival to human and non-human habitants. Dual power in the Anthropocene must be based on "ecological soviets" that guarantee the natural conditions of social reproduction.[17] As self-organizing collectivities of life, these ecological soviets have an autonomy capable of limiting the state and bringing about its eventual demise. These eco-soviets could lead as well to a system of the eco-social protection of life that would safeguard at once the wealth of biodiversity in natural ecosystems and public health standards for humans.

In certain respects, the mass unrest in Bolivia in 2019 and 2020 responded to the logic of dual power in that there was opposition between a progressive government that wanted to transform the state structure and multispecies commons united through various organizations, including the National Council of Ayllus and Markas of Qullasuyu. The anthropology of nature has recently turned to advocate for the cosmological weaving together of life (both human and nonhuman) in collectivities that are closed physically but that extend into a larger political sphere.[18] Their members possess land and cultivate it as a

---

16   Alberto Toscano, "After October, Before February: Figures of Dual Power," in Fredric Jameson, *An American Utopia: Dual Power and the Universal Army* (London: Verso, 2016), 405–58.

17   The idea of an "ecological soviet" comes from the unpublished work of Aimé Paris.

18   Philippe Descola, "Les usages de la terre. Cosmopolitiques de la territorialité," *Annuaire du Collège de France 2013–14*, 114/II (Paris: Collège de France, 2015), 757–81.

collectivity—proof that eco-soviets exist that could spur on a revolutionary transition and that act to balance state power. Without eco-soviets, it is difficult to imagine a balance of power that could constrain the state to take the necessary measures for an ecologically sustainable future. Eco-soviets would create a new organization of power by the reappropriation of the means of subsistence.

The transition to an ecologically sustainable future must first revise land ownership laws. We must abolish private ownership over the means of reproduction so as to liberate nature and to guarantee the conditions of subsistence of interspecific commons.[19] Yet the end of private property will not be enough to protect humans and nonhumans from catastrophes provoked by environmental degradation. Systems put in place to protect the public are vulnerable in ways linked to the destruction of wild habitats. At the same time, infectious diseases affecting farm animals (bird flu, mad cow disease) are exacerbated by industrial livestock production.

Once we admit the existence of a new climate regime, the question will be which type of politics will be effective for limiting the deleterious social and natural effects of our new reality. Disaster capitalism will make us confront something similar to what Rosa Luxemburg faced: socialism or barbarism; the dismantlement of wealth or the widespread destruction of life. Only an ecology of class—that is, a communism of life—will be able to protect the ecosphere.

---

19   Sarah Vanuxem, *La Propriété de la terre* (Marseille: Wildproject, 2018).

Acknowledgments

A book is always the singular trace of a cooperative effort. I had the good fortune of completing a large part of my research in the very open framework of the Sophiapol Laboratory at the Université Paris Nanterre, with the supervision of Stéphane Haber. This work owes much to him. The journals *Période*, *Vacarme*, and *Après la revolution* provided venues for rich discussion. The collective Reprise de terres (Take Back the Land) aided me in developing and deepening my first lines of thought. The concepts in this book were shared time and again with those "happy few" who were always interested to read, ready to push back, and yet always ready to read another draft. Most of the ideas here were run by Frédéric Monferrand, who will recognize many of our conversations in these pages. All the published chapters benefitted from the generous reading and friendly advice of Zoé Carle, Juliette Farjat, Thibault Henneton, Matthieu Renault, Isabelle Saint-Saëns, Thierry Santurenne, Claire Thouvenot, and Zacharias Zoubir. I also benefitted from the support and criticism of Christophe Bonneuil, Sebastian Budgen, Pierre Charbonnier, Nikola Chesnais, Alexis Cukier, Davide Gallo Lassere, Émilie Hache, Daniel Hartley, Razmig Keucheyan, Catherine Larrère, Jade Lindgaard, Andreas Malm, Jason W. Moore, Aimé Paris, Zahia Rahmani, Tony Wood, and Xavier Wrona.

A book is also proof of the work of a publishing team, and I want to warmly thank Éditions Amsterdam for taking on this project. I am deeply grateful to Verso for the publication of the English version of *Terre et capital*, and to Matt Reeck, the translator, for his amazing work on both the philosophical argument of the book and writing style. I owe a great debt of gratitude as well to Élisabeth and Edmond Guillibert for their commitment to my education. Finally, I would like to thank Lucie-Lou Pignot, who never lets me forget that the true philosopher makes light of philosophy.

Index

Adorno, Theodor W., 121
Anderson, Kevin B., 69
Anderson, Perry, 59
Andrade, Luis Martínez, 133, 147, 148
Anievas, Alexander, 73–4
Aricó, José, 133, 136–7, 139, 142
Aristotle, 54–5, 79–80
Audier, Serge, 5, 13, 82
Axelrod, Pavel, 70

Bakunin, Mikhail, 62, 64–5, 67
Balaud, Léna, 34, 174
Ballard, James Graham, 10
Becker, Marc, 147
Bernstein, Henry, 124
Billington, James, 64, 76, 82
Bloch, Ernst, 23, 128–31, 148–59, 163, 167–8
Bonneuil, Christophe, 11, 187
Bookchin, Murray, 6

Brenner, Robert, 14, 39
Burkett, Paul, 86
Butler, Judith, 24, 47, 91
Byres, Terence J., 124

Carle, Zoé, 120
Castro Pozo, Hildebrando, 141–2, 145
Charbonneau, Bernard, 6
Charbonnier, Pierre, 30, 122, 178
Chayanov, Alexander, 61
Chernychevsky, Nikolay, 59, 62–3, 82
Chopot, Antoine, 34, 174
Crabbe, George, 102–4
Cronon, William, 33, 57, 91
Cowley, Abraham, 102

Danielson, Nikolay, 59, 66–8, 84
De Santis, Sergio, 142–3, 145
Descola, Philippe, 25, 53, 169, 185

Di Chiro, Giovanna, 11
Dickens, Charles, 110–12
Dolci, Paula, 120

Ellul, Jacques, 6
Engels, Friedrich, 5, 11–12, 16–17,
    28–31, 39–40, 66–9, 70, 84, 88,
    110, 123–30, 172
Estes, Nick, 21–3

Ferdinand, Malcolm, 20
Fischbach, Franck, 52–3
Foster, John Bellamy, 86
France, Anatole, ix
Fraas, Karl, 59
Frémeaux, Isabelle, 26
Fressoz, Jean-Baptiste, 3, 11

Galeano, Eduardo, 132
Gilio-Whitaker, Dina, 21
Graber, Frédéric, 38
Godelier, Maurice, 39–40, 50, 96–7
Goldsmith, Oliver, 102
Gunder Frank, André, 132
Gutiérrez Merino, Gustavo, 148

Haber, Stéphane, 24, 91
Habermas, Jürgen, 24, 91, 149
Haraway, Donna, 31
Hartley, Daniel, 96, 101, 105, 112, 118,
    187
Harvey, David, 15
Hecht, Gabrielle, 176
Hermitte, Marie-Angèle, 169
Herzen, Alexander, 62–3

Hobsbawm, Eric, 12, 39
Horkheimer, Max, 121
Hunt, Tristam, 67

Ingold, Alice, 164

Jonson, Ben, 106–7
Jordan, Jay, 26

Keucheyan, Razmig, 21, 133
Kirkpatrick, Sale, 121
Klein, Naomi, 179
Kovalevsky, Maksim, 59

Lavrov, Pyotr, 59, 84
Latour, Bruno, 5, 12, 122, 172
Lefebvre, Henri, 7
Le Guin, Ursula, ix
Lenin, Vladimir I., 39–40, 76, 81, 124,
    183–4
Leopold, Aldo, 27
Liebig, Justus von, 44, 59, 83–6
Lindner, Kolja, 59, 61
Locher, Fabien, 38
Loraux, Nicole, 126
Löwy, Michael, 95, 112, 121, 136–7, 142,
    149, 161–2
Luxemburg, Rosa, 186

Malm, Andreas, 9, 11, 120, 179
Mariátegui, José Carlos, 119, 123,
    133–49, 157–68
Martínez Alier, Joan, 59–60
Marx, Karl, 1, 2, 5, 7, 11–13, 16, 18, 19,
    29, 31, 36, 38, 39, 40, 41, 42, 44–61,

65–89, 94–7, 116, 123, 131, 133–8, 143, 172–3, 175, 181, 183

Merchant, Carolyn, 37–8

Mikhaylosky, Nikolay, 62–4, 68, 75, 76

Mitchell, Timothy, 178

Miroshevski, Vladimir, 133, 135, 141–2

Monferrand, Frédéric, 30, 57

Moore, Jason W., 11, 34, 57

Morizot, Baptiste, 122

Morris, William, 76, 95

Münster, Arno, 159

Müntzer, Thomas, 125, 127–9, 172

Nişancoğlu, Kerem, 73

Omrod, David, 73

Paris, Aimé, 185

Paris, Robert, 135, 145

Perrin, Coline, 120

Plekhanov, Gueorgui, 70

Quijano, Aníbal, 160

Rolston III, Holmes, 26

Saito, Kohei, 44–6

Sand, Shlomo, 164

Shanin, Teodor, 59, 61–2, 63, 64, 77–8, 82, 123

Solón, Pablo, 170

Sorel, Georges, 133, 143, 163–6

Stengers, Isabelle, 3–4

Tanuro, Daniel, 176

Tönnies, Ferdinand, 137

Toscano, Alberto, 185

Tsing, Anna Lowenhaupt, 33

Vanden, Harry, 147

Vanuxem, Sarah, 186

Venturi, Franco, 62–3, 66, 67, 70

Vernadsky, Vladimir, 61

Viveiros de Castro, Eduardo, 9, 34

Volodine, Antoine, 36

Weber, Max, 146, 153–4

Westholm, Hilmar, 44

Williams, Raymond, 90, 92–109, 112–18, 123

Wood, Ellen Meiksins, 39, 72

Zasulich, Vera, 59, 70–1, 82–3, 84, 86–8, 123, 124, 136

Zetkin Collective, 11, 120, 179